WHAT OTHERS ARE SAYING

Controlling the mind and directing it is a great challenge. With the help of this wonderful book, "*Pick-of-the-Day!*" along with the set of cards, it's a great help in living a beautiful, peaceful and prosperous life.

- *Terry Cole-Whittaker,* Author
Live Your Bliss; Dare to be Great; How to Have More in a Have Not World; What You Think of Me is None of My Business

Dr. Mary Anderson's book "*Pick-of-the-Day!*" presents well written, easy to understand practical wisdom for living a happier, healthier and more meaningful life:

- *Margrit Spear, PhD/MFT,* Author
*Life Changing Explosion of Consciousness,
Introduction to Holographic Psychology*

The value of Dr. Anderson's book establishes the communication between the doctor and patient to reinforce and respect Innate within for self-growth, creativity and an image to enhance a vitalistic approach to better health and well-being

*Dr. Guy R. Riekeman, D.C.,*President
Life University, Marietta GA

I highly recommend "*Pick-of-the-Day!*" by Dr. Mary B. Anderson, for both reading and practice. Dr. Anderson masterfully integrates her own experiences of healing and as a healer with the wisdom of the Ages, and combines that with an elegantly simple method to connect to our Innate oneness with Nature via the "randomicity" of the universe. When we choose her "pick cards" we feel the connection with being. And, happily, as to the physics of how this sort of thing works, Dr. Anderson gets it right when she writes, "Unfortunately, though, it is not fully explainable." This is a method to be lived.

- *Thomas G. Brophy, PhD,* Author
*The Mechanism Demands a Mysticism;
The Origin Map; Black Genesis*

Dr. Mary Anderson's *"Pick-of-the-Day!"* is a reflection of this wonderful insightful healer. Her intuitive skills demonstrate that she has practiced the Innate truths revealed in her book. After reading the book and following the suggested course of action, the cards seemed to reveal the Creator's purpose for the day. Taking time to use this tool will open emotional/spiritual insights that are often overlooked or suppressed in a busy day's activity. I urge everyone to read the book and enjoy the game of life God has given us to play.

> - *Dan O. Harper, M.D.*, Boarded Family Physician and Holistic Physician, Solana Beach CA

We are all subconsciously aware of our connection to a greater presence. As health professionals we tend to forget that treating patients is so much more than discovering a diagnosis and rendering treatment. The founders of chiropractic were acutely aware of this connection. They called it the Innate. However, in the quest for acceptance in the allopathic and scientific communities, this awareness has been frequently disregarded and ignored, if not lost. Mary Anderson, one of chiropractic's true healers, has once again illuminated the path to the Innate in her book "*Pick of the Day!*" Thank you for leading us back to impart the essence of practicing a healing art.

> - *Deborah Pate, D.C., D.A.C.B.R.*
> Columnist for *Dynamic Chiropractic*™, co-author of *Case Studies in Chiropractic Radiology* and practicing chiropractic radiologist

Dr. Mary Anderson's book, "*Pick-of-the-Day!*" is terrific for self discovery! Her years of experience allowed her to laser into thirty pertinent topics that are relevant for everyone. Her in-depth decades of practice have led her to knowing how to make transformative ideas simple. Her creative pictorial approach makes reading her book not only life changing but fun.

> - *Reverend Christian Sorensen, D.D.*
> Spiritual Leader of Seaside Center for Spiritual Living
> Author of: *Soar, Catch the Spirit, Riding the Waves of Life; A Book of Prayers, Good Cents; Free Your Own Tibet;* co-authored *Joyous Freedom Journal*

Pick-of-the-Day!

Life is like a game and it's all about how to Innately play it!

Activities for Self-Empowerment

A COMPLETE HOME STUDY COURSE
By
Dr. Mary B. Anderson

Companion Publishers™
Encinitas, California
USA

Copyright ©2009 by Dr. Mary B. Anderson
All rights reserved.

ISBN: 978-0-9842719-0-0
Library of Congress Control Number: 2009910543

Published by Companion Publishers™
Encinitas, California

This book is protected by United States and international copyright law, including electronic and Internet copyright laws. The contents may not be used, reproduced, translated or published in any form, including printed, electronic or any other media without the expressed written permission of the Author.

Except by written agreement, no part of this publication may be reproduced, stored in a retrieval system or transmitted in any form or by any means, electronic, mechanical, recording or otherwise, without prior permission on behalf of the copyright holders. Any use of this material to target advertising or similar activities is explicitly forbidden and may be a cause for prosecution.

This book is for anyone who wishes to explore daily living from a new awareness of how their own Innate Intelligence reflects both their outer and inner worlds. Even though the topics resulted from treating patients and the common threads observed, you don't have to be under any patient/doctor relationship to recognize many of the subjects presented for self-empowerment.

Dear Reader,

Thank you for purchasing PICK-OF-THE-DAY!

This home study course consists of the workbook text. A deck of cards is recommended to be used in conjunction with each topic. The cards are designed to assist you with daily empowerment activities.

Card options include:
1. Order a deck of cards from TreasuresFromMary.com.
2. Purchase a deck of cards via regular mail by using the order form in the back of book.
3. Have your Daily Card electronically selected via the card generator at TreasuresFromMary.com
4. Make your own cards using blank index or business size cards. Each topic illustrates what to put on the card.

Know that LIFE IS A LIKE A GAME AND IT'S ALL ABOUT HOW TO INNATELY PLAY IT! I wish you a very happy experience putting the concept and exercises in this book to work in your life.

I originally wanted the book printed with multiple color pages. The cost would have been prohibitive unless I outsourced the printing to a foreign country. I chose black and white to keep this work designed and printed in the U.S.A.

Best Wishes,

Dr. Mary B. Anderson

Dedication

To my husband Don, whose understanding and loyal support provided me with the freedom to practice the art and science of chiropractic so that I may lovingly be of service to my patients.

*Recognize and claim your
Innate Intelligence.*

*It can never be separated from
Universal Intelligence.*

Therein lies your power!

CONTENTS

Dear Reader	vii
Dedication	ix
Epigraph	xi
Table of Contents	xiii
Preface	xvii

PART I – Open the Door to Innate

Chapter 1	Life is like a game and it's all about how to Innately play it!	1
Chapter 2	And…What is Innate?	7
Chapter 3	Treat Innate with Respect	15
Chapter 4	Believing in Innate Reveals Wisdom	23

PART II – Pick-of-the-Day!

How to Use Part II 33

List of 30 topics
(in numerical order)

List of 30 topics
(in alphabetical order)

Open Your Eyes	39	Attitude	77
Criticism	43	Awareness	83
Look for the Good	47	Be Receptive	87
Patience	51	Comfort	115
Light	55	Contentment	139

List of 30 topics (in numerical order)		List of 30 topics (in alphabetical order)	
Food for Thought	59	Control	67
Evenness	63	Courage	95
Control	67	Criticism	43
Gratefulness	71	Decision Making	123
Habits	75	Evenness	63
Attitude	77	Food for Thought	59
Responsibility	81	Gratefulness	71
Awareness	83	Growing Pains	91
Be Receptive	87	Habits	75
Growing Pains	91	Intuition	151
Courage	95	Keep it to Yourself	111
Understanding	99	Kindness	107
Wisdom	103	Laughing	135
Kindness	107	Light	55
Keep it to Yourself	111	Look for the Good	47
Comfort	115	Open Your Eyes	39
Trust	119	Patience	51
Decision Making	123	Peace	147
Priorities	127	Priorities	127
Undesired Project	131	Responsibility	81
Laughing	135	Stillness	143
Contentment	139	Trust	119
Stillness	143	Understanding	99
Peace	147	Undesired Project	131
Intuition	151	Wisdom	103

Appendix A: Sample of completed chart   *155*
Blank Chart to Tally Card Selections   *157*

PART III – Self-Talk

How to Use Part III   *161*

WHAT ARE YOU SAYING TO YOURSELF   *163*
   We cannot get away from ourselves
      no matter where we go   *165*
   What we think and say determines
      life's experiences   *171*
   How to identify feelings both in and
      out of your comfort zone   *177*
   How to talk to yourself   *183*

Acknowledgements   *193*
Bibliography   *195*
Disclaimer   *197*
Order Form   *199*
Card Description   *203*
About the Author   *205*

PREFACE

My quest is daring you to believe in yourself. The Self is the most empowering gift we have. It has transcended me to a renewed life and the lives of so many people that have embodied their own introspection.

In my twenties, I was plagued with illnesses that seemed unrelenting. Being a migraine sufferer for 11 years, having asthma, gallbladder dysfunction, and uterine bleeding, which lasted eighteen days every month for two years, I felt forced into seeking alternative health. I was one of those patients who did not respond successfully to conventional approaches.

My first introduction to the body/mind connection came from my mentor and chiropractor, Dr. Ronald C. Pluese. He took a special interest in my welfare and taught me how thoughts play a major role in recovery. More than that, with the philosophy of chiropractic in knowing that we have an Innate Intelligence within, a whole new understanding of being connected to a spiritual power unfolded. Not an entity separate from us, but a spiritual Intelligence that indwells in us that knows that it knows. **Part I** introduces Innate in ways that are built into our "gut feelings" and why this incredible Intelligence doesn't ever go away. Once that understanding is made a part of our awareness, treating this Innate with respect has more value than our intellectual mind can fathom, thereby, a Wisdom flourishes and one may wonder where it comes from, but not to worry, it's inexhaustible. Unfortunately, though, it is not fully explainable. I chose to use this Innate Wisdom when I was ultimately diagnosed with cancer in 1976. I will talk more about those results in Chapter 4.

Several years later, Dr. Pluese's impact on my life inspired me to become a chiropractor. I wanted to emulate this wonderful enlightened doctor, but it was more than that. I wanted to serve mankind and help others to awaken within themselves the connection that saved my life. Connecting with that Innate Intelligence gave me the power, the motivation, and perseverance needed to choose a path for which I am eternally grateful.

I've been practicing since 1982 and have seen in patients a replica of many challenges I had experienced. *Pick-of-the-Day!* was developed as a result of the accompanying commonalities, which were uncovered after treating the "chief complaints" of patients. Since we cannot separate body, mind and spirit, many chronic and recurrent conditions are complicated by a mental/emotional component. Teaching patients to look at their thoughts during periods when they are experiencing symptoms has opened up to them the relationship between the body and mind.

The topics in **Part II** are <u>not</u> so devastating as to seek out professional counseling. The topics are about dealing with everyday circumstances so that when they are brought to your attention, the awareness can be helpful in increasing your quality of life. The goal is to become a more balanced individual; in other words, to help alleviate daily stressors and find ways to grow.

Individual commonalities have been made into a deck of cards. The *Pick-of-the-Day!* cards are not affirmations. They are much more and include an activity associated with them to either do and/or contemplate. This brings in the element of spirit, the inner voice that contains the Innate Intelligence we inherited as part of the creative process.

Since circumstances and habits have a way of repeating themselves, *Pick-of-the-Day!* helps to bring to your attention what is emphasized by what card you draw regularly.

Part III takes you through the process of teaching you to self-evaluate how your thinking may relate to your body's signs and symptoms while experiencing them, or immediately following a set of circumstances. It's a tool for life-long introspections. Keep in mind *that every chronic physical problem has a mental component.*

How to Use Part II and Part III can be found in the beginning of those sections. (That's right! To get the most out of this book, there is homework.)

My intention in writing this book is to reach more people and to awaken more fully to that inner voice, that consciousness that empowers you to know what feels right to you. It is my belief that we all know the difference of what works and does not work on an individual basis. It's a Wisdom that I refer to in Chapters 2, 3, & 4. If this whets your appetite, read more about these subjects in related books found in the bibliography.

Working with the body/mind connection far surpasses just reading about how it works. You are gifted with a spirit underlying your ego self. The spirit is that part of you that precedes the acquired you. The acquired you is what you have become through the development of the self from lifestyle, habits, educational and/or environmental influences. It's how you have lived your life up to this point.

Dr. Mary B. Anderson

Encinitas, California

PART I

OPEN THE DOOR TO INNATE

CHAPTER ONE

> **Pick-of-the-Day!**
>
> *Life is like a game and it's all about how to Innately play it!*

We all participate in life from the level of our understanding. That's why the playing fields may be different for everyone. However, before we know it, we are placed in a world that is governed by rules and regulations. Many of these rules are meant for our safety and rightly so, otherwise our day-to-day living in general would be in chaos. Order is needed in a civilized community. Keeping time brings about organization and schedules. Without time we would have to depend on chance for conducting business. In order to get the most out of our day, we have been taught time management skills. The external world we live in becomes dependent on how well we make decisions, communicate, organize, manage money and function with appropriate behavior.

We watch TV and take in all the "awfuls", with a small percentage of uplifting stories. These observations lead us to believe that almost everyone breaks the rules and regulations that have been formulated in this external world, which ideally is meant to live in unity or harmony. The external world seems to be dependent on actions and reactions that may or may not be under our direct control. The human race has evolved into the consciousness that points fingers and blames others showing little accountability or responsibility, instead turning themselves into victims. Of course, all of these examples come from being an observer. It also depends on where you have placed yourself in the midst of this external world as outcomes are observed.

How can we turn a deaf ear to this external world and still hear what is going on around us? It takes playing the game of life from a different point of view and developing our internal world to that of self-discovery.

Personal choices have determined the situations we are now experiencing, and personal choices can lead us to participate in this external game of life through a perspective that is being governed by our internal reality.

We have been taught from early childhood what's right and wrong and have been expected to abide by what others have said. Many points of view are wonderful and good, which have developed into needed guidelines. As we mature, those voices that have directed us start to stir up our own sanity checks from within. In other words, we question what is right and wrong from our self-developed level of understanding.

This appears to be a natural unfoldment. It takes us out of the intellectual decision making process of how things ought to be and puts us in the place of knowingness about ourselves. It is going back to the involution of our mind. What does that really mean? It means that there is a part of us that knows that it knows. It's that inherent part of us that has been inherited by right of our spiritual origin. It is part and parcel of that Universal Intelligence that expresses our Innate Intelligence. In simple language, it is "our gut feeling". All the rest of how we think and act as a result of rules and regulations have evolved through or because of language, survival, community, and/or government.

Confucius acknowledged these developmental stages 2500 years ago, so this is not new to our times. The teachings of Confucius give us the direction of knowing that our conscience lets us know that we know. That's a powerful understanding. This understanding helps us to function in unity and harmony in our external reality, which is directed by our internal reality.

There are two kinds of self-knowledge: the true Self and the ego self. The true Self is originated in the Mind of what created us in the first place. That makes us a co-creator by our very thoughts. That part of our Self needs to be differentiated from the ego self, resulting from a compilation of the thinking processes through the ages. It has developed as a result of the evolution of thought. It is the evolution of the human race consciousness that gives us what we see in the external world.

When we quiet our minds of all the chatter that goes on and eliminate all the options that are running through our brains, we come to a place where we empty our thoughts. Buddha referred to this as "no mind". It's a place where this involution takes place. Involution precedes evolution.

Many of the great sages and mystics have gone to that place in consciousness and have experienced insights which bring us back to Oneness, the Self, the origin of what and who we are. Much like how our modern day physicists are searching for the origins of what may have preceded the Big Bang.

Maybe we can look at the Big Bang as our own discovery of who and what we are because that is a Big Bang within our own minds. It's an awakening to that Innate Intelligence that knows that it knows.

This concept allows us to play this game of life with a deck of cards that helps us to unfold by questioning our thoughts, reactions, feelings and emotions. The evolution into form is our body language. It has a unique way of expressing itself through pain and suffering. Buddha tells us that the cause of suffering is not the change itself, but the human desire to hold on to the things that keep them from changing.

In the Christian teachings, Jesus tells us that "I of myself can do nothing. It is the Father within that doeth the works." That same Father which is within each and every one of us. It allows us to be a co-creator.

The Kabbalah teaches one to bring in more light to overcome the darkness.

It doesn't seem to matter what approach one takes. Lao Tzu, the great Chinese Taoist philosopher states, "There are many paths to the top of the mountain, and when you get there the view is all the same." The only guide, which leads you to the place of this clear vision, is your own Innate Intelligence. Ram Dass, in his book *Journey of Awakening (1978),* tells us that, "After you arrive at the summit, after going through the total transformation of being, after becoming free of fear, doubt, confusion, and self-consciousness, there is yet one more step to the completion of that journey: the return to the valley below, to the everyday world. Who it is that returns is not who began the climb in the first place. The being that comes back is quietness itself, is compassion and wisdom, is the truth of the ages. Whatever humble or elevated position that being holds within the community, he or she becomes a light for others on the way, a statement of the freedom that comes from having touched the top of the mountain."

In the final analysis it is our perception of what we have discovered that counts. It is vital that you have a basic understanding about the Innate within you. It is **"the most**

important aspect!" I know that I can count on that Innate Intelligence to reveal your Truth. If you never find your own Innate you will never know what can be revealed. If you do find your Innate, participating in the lower realms or regions of the external world, will not be the same after reaching the top of the summit. Of course, there is no money back guarantee. Why? Because it is free.

CHAPTER TWO

And…What is Innate?

Innate Intelligence is the spirit in the body/mind/spirit connection. It's the unknown factor that knows that it knows. Everyone has experienced the unknown factor, like knowing that someone is going to call you on the phone, or sensing an accident or telepathic communication. ESP (extrasensory perception) has been demonstrated over and over again, but still cannot be explained by present day physics. Even hard-core scientists follow hunches.

How I interpret Innate Intelligence may be a stretch for you. Others may already have adopted their own ideas for themselves. However, a concrete definition of Innate Intelligence as part of the Universal Intelligence, or a First Cause (being the cause of all things) would infer limitations so it still remains the greatest mystery of all times. Intellectualizing this Intelligence has been the quest of the human race since recorded history. This search includes questions of "Who am I?" "Where did I come from?" "Where am I going?" These questions have been posed by the greatest philosophers and scientists in search for life's answers. What we have all around us is the effect of both Universal and Innate Intelligence. The creator with all its co-creators (no matter how you internalize it) has manifested what we see around us in solid form.

Whether you believe in the Big Bang theory, or the story of creation in the Biblical Book of Genesis, or join in the continued inquiries of the gods as told in the Vedas, or whatever your mind can conceive, the mystery of creation has yet to be solved. In any event, there is an evolutionary process that cannot be denied. The biggest question continues to remain, "How and when did it all begin?" The origin of the universe contains the greatest secrets of the ages. The very thought can mentally challenge the minds of what one believes. Thoughts and ideas have been compared from eras long past to those of the present and there is still confusion in the mind. There have been shifts in how we see the universe and on a microscopic level on how our own personal universe fits into the big scheme of things. The search to understand how all this new science fits in with the transformational process of a belief system leads one to depend on their own intuitive abilities. Why? Probably because our feelings and emotions have validity built into them, which there haven't been adequate words yet to describe. Maybe a new vocabulary will be forthcoming with the advent of consciousness studies.

Some find it questions their spiritual and religious beliefs to accept a more scientific outlook or study. Some minds stop there, and some minds have come back full circle to their original belief systems with a different outlook. Others come full circle by way of a Möbius strip where their beliefs intertwine and cannot be differentiated. Life is a real journey. Whatever level your beliefs are is where your own consciousness will resonate. The exercises given in this book on *What are you saying to yourself* and the *Pick of-the-Day!* topics made into cards are all meant for introspection and to see what level your life is operating at. As time goes by, your views and answers may change like the weather. The wind is like a gust that flows through you. It is full of vitality with all its fluctuations. It's the life force you cannot see, but is there. We see the effects of the wind, and the rain provides nourishment bringing what is needed to grow. Eventually if you search deep enough to connect with your own Innate, you will find a growing experience where there are no descriptive words in our language to relate to what you will discover within.

In the newest proposed theory in science, Brian Greene describes vibrational dimensions known as string theory in his books, *The Elegant Universe (1999)* and *Fabric of the Cosmos (2004)*. We have all experienced the "vibes" of one type or another. It's the same as the vibrational levels of what the mystics, sages and philosophers have experienced to bring into their reality.

Rather than beating our brains out with the origins of this Innate Intelligence, the effects of this Intelligence has given us a more realistic understanding for the materialistic mind to accept.

But, what about that part of us that knows that it knows, and doesn't have anything tangible to display yet? I admire the great men of science. Everyone one of them had to start with a thought, which eventually led to great discoveries. Many of their thoughts came from an intuition and those scientists had the courage to follow what their unknown world was telling them.

We can list some of the great minds in science and their contributions. What we must not forget is that they are people who have had everyday experiences just like you and me. Many of their laboratories just happen to be in big buildings, with big money projects. Their minds have and are still searching for the Truth to the same questions the mystics and sages have internalized for answers.

The thoughts of an Innate Intelligence cannot be denied whether one is an atheist, an agnostic or believes in a god. Why? Because everything that goes back to its origin has an evolutionary unfoldment that has to lead to something including us. We cannot deny we are part of this process. Simple things we take for granted like the healing of a cut finger or the complexity of fetal development tells us that we have an Innate Intelligence.

Aside from the confirming physical sciences of mathematics, chemistry and biology, bold steps have changed the minds of numerous physicists to accept the theories of relativity, quantum mechanics, and now venturing into string theory adding multiple dimensions to life itself. We are not there yet, but we are getting closer and closer to a grand unified field theory. This very dream that Albert Einstein held onto until the day he died. His famous quote, "God does not play dice with the Universe" has haunted many minds. In actuality this statement came about because Einstein had a disbelief in quantum physics and the Copenhagen interpretation that brought about the belief that events in nature were purely random. Einstein was convinced that there was a Oneness behind the Universe and that non-deterministic parts were very relevant.

Oneness of all life started to surface in the Rig-Veda 10:129. These hymns were sung by the sages of India and thought to be one of the first to describe the origins of the universe when the idea of ASAT (non-existent) or SAT (existent) was born out of spontaneity. This monism became an accepted principle because the beliefs in many gods did not answer the cries of the great thinkers of that time period.

The sages tell us that there was darkness at the beginning and that a force was hidden by a shell, and that One was born through the power of its own heat.

This description sounds much like the origin of the universe which scientists now believe is approximately 14 billion years old. The Rig-Veda was written approximately 1200 B.C.E.

From this monistic view it was believed that anyone who knew this Oneness about themselves and the Universe could conquer the world.

On a grand scale science has found natural laws to work with and has been able to build bridges, fly planes, and even venture to other planets. On the same scale, when we also believe that we are part of this master plan, like the sages of long ago, we can find the secrets to help us live our life from the inside out.

Think about your own definition of Innate Intelligence. I remember many years ago, a very old chiropractor asked me to define Innate. I thought I would be very thorough in my explanation. He kept asking me, "And what else?" In sheer frustration of not giving him the answer he wanted, I blurted out, "Innate is 100%!" His response was, "Never forget that."

It has taken me decades of studying science and comparative religions to see and understand what my patients have expressed in their physical symptoms and their relationship to their belief systems. I have taken a long walk around the Möbius strip because there is no getting off at any stops. Innate is never going to go away. You may as well get used to it. It's your inner friend for life. You won't find it out there somewhere; you will only find it within!

From my own personal experience and in the experiences I have had with patient care, it is through the integration of body/mind/spirit that physical and mental health transcends into a wellness. When one accepts the role of this integration, outcomes are better and long lasting. As minds transcend and connect with their Innate Intelligence experiences go beyond physical recovery and a material reality. Personalities expand with an awareness in decision making with clarity permeating their mental well being. Healings take place. Many of these experiences were deep enough that it questioned their previous belief structures. I ask, "Are you ready for the Big Bang?"

CHAPTER THREE

Treat Innate with Respect

Years ago as a child I was taught that "we are temples of the Holy Spirit". Did I really know what that meant? It sounded mysterious to me, but at the same time I felt special because I was told the Holy Spirit resided in me.

As I continued to walk my Möbius strip path, where there is no getting off and there are no stops, I kept going and going like the "Energizer Bunny" searching for what made sense to me. I began to realize that being a temple of the Holy Spirit is just a religious way of saying that our body vehicle has that spark of life I now identify as Innate Intelligence, which is born of the Universal Intelligence (or the Holy Spirit). It's the essence of who we are at the core level of everything in existence (SAT) that comes from that which was non-existent (ASAT).

Science tells us that our atoms were created from stars through explosions and supernovas that form in the solar system, and now we are part of that same solar system.

No matter what your belief system is, there's a part of us that reflects the non-existent to the existence and it won't go away.

In recalling the past, I'm sure you have posed a similar question, "How do I fit into this picture of life?" There may be no specific answer, but there may be a "gut" response that tells you the answer is somewhere to be found within yourself.

This Innate creates an inherent search for a deeper philosophical understanding, which also has a brain science component built into human biology. In any event, the journey is transforming. As Andrew Newberg, M.D. says in his book *Why God Won't Go Away* (2001), it is "...a journey of self discovery toward which I believe our brain compels us."

Two researchers, Andrew Newberg, M.D. and Eugene D'Aguili, M.D., Ph.D. did a study in an attempt to find any connection between human consciousness and the persistent longing to identify with a power greater than oneself. They wanted something to measure, which would validate this Innate drive and verify it within scientific parameters.

Two groups of subjects were chosen for the research. One group consisted of Tibetan monks who believed that during their meditative process they were *uniting* with the Oneness of all creation. (This meant there was no separation from that Oneness).The other group were Franciscan nuns at prayer. The nuns would describe the closeness of *co-mingling* with God. (This meant there was a separation from God). At a key moment in the subject's connection with this elevated state in consciousness, radioactive material was injected into the veins of the subject. A

SPECT camera (single photon emission computed tomography) would scan the brain to detect the pathway and location of the radioactive tracer.

The imaging of the SPECT scan showed normal neurological activity prior to this heightened meditative or religious state; however, during their peak moments in an elevated state the neurological activity had a sharp reduction. The mystical experience is scientifically real as observed in this biological experiment.

There have been studies where meditation has reduced blood pressure, pulse rates, and muscle activity in relaxation that can be measured, but this experiment reached a different level – that of the central nervous system. Newberg and D'Aguili have concluded human biology compels the spiritual urge and their hypothesis was reached by sifting through religious experiences, rituals and brain science that emerged meaningful patterns. If this subject intrigues you, as it did me, I suggest you read *Why God Won't Go Away (2001)*.

Does this research challenge one's faith in any religious sect? I would have to say that if anything, it strengthens the entire concept of a Universal Intelligence and that our own Innate Intelligence is ever more real. Back to that walk on the Möbuis strip.

I read a book that took me "forever" to get through. *Mysticism* (1910), a classic written by Evelyn Underhill and it absolutely fascinated me to read about the profound spiritual and religious experiences of the saints in medieval times. Their paths of service may have been different, but ultimately their Oneness with God was described in a similar fashion.

Studying the life of the Siddhartha Gautama, who became a Buddha, tells the same story of an urge that was seeking answers to why there was so much suffering in the human experience.

The Christian philosophy and teachings of Jesus, the Christ, can be summarized in the *Sermon on the Mount*.

It's interesting that the descriptive definitions of Buddha and Christ have the same meaning – The Enlightened One.

The dream of the Grand Unified Field Theory without compromise is what Einstein yearned for in his lifetime. The search for the unknown areas which gave great scientists like Galileo, Kepler, Newton, Faraday, Maxwell, Planck, Bohr and many more, the impetus which came from a transcendence within their own minds to seek levels of understanding which continually have no apparent end.

What is happening here is that we all have the same Innate drive to expand our human awareness to seek self-discovery, which is inherent within.

There's a part of each one of us that has this sense of perception. The perception that knows within one's self what takes us out of our "comfort zone". It's a part of us that puts us on a transformational journey whether we realize it or not. Once we can step back and be the observer of what our life looks like, the game of life can take on a more meaningful approach without such a strenuous effort because our own Innate Intelligence can be in the driver's seat. Some people choose to be in battle with themselves. When they finally realize that their strongest ally is to be found within themselves the awakening emerges.

Whether you believe in the evolutionary process based on a scientific explanation or the creation story of any of the major philosophies or religions, the one thing in common is that our neural systems conduct under the same principles whether it be a worm or a human, the differences is in the complexity of the species. The chemical and electrical stimulations follow natural law. This natural law follows the Universal Intelligence that is within the minds of scientists, religious and/or philosophical sages or prophets and you. We are all expressing in a language that resonates to our personal motivation and interests.

It's exciting to realize that our basic functions do not have to be orchestrated. It's all part of the master plan. It's when that master plan has gone awry that we want to control it from outside sources. The question is, "Are we more intelligent than the Intelligence that made us?" Granted, we all need help along the way and many turn over this direction to someone else because we have more faith in others, forgetting that we need to also take an active role. Unfortunately, comments from patients after going from one physician to another have been, "Well, that's what I'm paying him for. I'm still not better." That should be a wake-up call that money doesn't buy everything! Answers are not always in a pill, surgery, rehabilitation, physical therapy or any other modality. They may help us to control or get rid of pain; however, personal responsibility is paramount. True healing comes from integrating the body/mind/spirit connection.

I've been at the bedside of people dying of cancer and they tell me they have been healed because they cleared their minds to be in that "comfort zone" and forgave themselves and others, thereby releasing their consciousness to enter into transition without resistance. That may be an extreme case while being on a deathbed, but are we not dying one day at a time? Celebrating life with your best foot forward allows one to go through the process with joy, peace, harmony and love knowing that you are perceiving life from the highest point of view. Remember our brains operate through the science of perception.

Science does understand that we have perceptive abilities, but one thing that is still puzzling is how this awareness got there in the first place. In fact, that's the same struggle the philosophical minds have been trying to solve. What is known for sure is that we think, have emotions, experience sensations, have intuitions and all this is labeled as "mind". This part of us does influence the body and how our physiology can change as a result of our thinking. The search continues for why it works within ourselves. All things in nature have a built-in intelligence even though it is not always easily seen on a macroscopic level. Until we can integrate body, mind and spirit consciously our lives are fragmented. The wholeness of what we really are…is seeking the expression it was designed to express.

Altered states of consciousness, as previously noted in the SPECT scan studies, does show that the mind has the ability to experience mystical states. These mystical states are where many of the great innovative thoughts were established. It's where answers to difficult problems have been solved, and where the religions of the world found their origins. More importantly, it is also where we resonate to what feels right to each and every one of us. These altered states seem to take us back to our origin because it empties our mind and thoughts. We may never truly understand how it works, but it does work, so work with it. What is known is that this spirit part of us takes the thought and forms an image. With this image it creates. It's the same energy used to solidify the particles, protons, electrons, atoms, and molecules into substance that materializes. What a wonderful power we possess! Look around your space right now. Every single object started the same way. Your life and the outcomes were created in the same way. It all starts with spirit -or- what is unseen. Infuse your mind and your thoughts with what you want to manifest. Everything follows the same natural laws and principles.

> The development of intuition [spirit] as partner of intellect [mind], science as partner with being [consciousness], can only lead to hope and to freedom.
>
> Thomas G. Brophy, Ph.D.
> *The Mechanism Demands a Mysticism, An Exploration of Spirit, Matter and Physics (1999)*

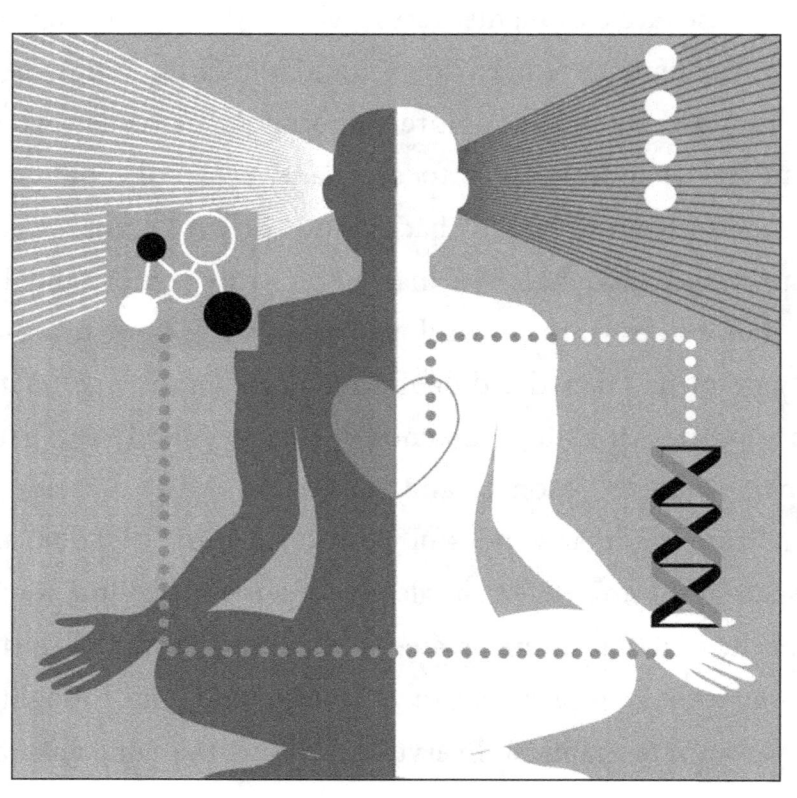

CHAPTER FOUR

Believing in Innate Reveals Wisdom

It is no longer necessary to be a "doubting Thomas" as to whether all this Innate stuff works. Interesting research in cell biology was done by Bruce Lipton, Ph.D. in a new science known as Epigenetics. In his book, *The Biology of Belief, unleashing the power of consciousness, matter and miracles* (2005), Dr. Lipton defined epigenetics as the study of molecular mechanisms by which the environment controls gene activity. That's right, cellular communication determines our fate and not necessarily our genes.

It is exciting to be able to believe and understand the Wisdom of Innate Intelligence and that it responds to the aforementioned "collective consciousness". I encourage you to read Dr Lipton's book. It answered for me why and how I had the most profound health experiences of my life.

As a result of familial history, I was totally convinced that fate had endowed me with a "crappy set of genes". How else could I explain 11 years of migraines, difficulty breathing from asthma, and ultimately being diagnosed with cervical cancer? My aunts, grandmother and mother had them all! This was really hard to believe because the religion I was born into stated, "we are made in the image and likeness of God". I challenged these bodily dysfunctions and refused to believe that God would give me all those illnesses if I were truly made in His image. Personal enlightenment came as a result of accepting the concept of having perfect cells that knew what and how to live in harmony within this "dragged down" body. The struggle was a long one, but I was persistent. To make a long story short, there was a remarkable spontaneous cancer remission in 1976, the evening before scheduled surgery. Prior to my cancer diagnosis, the migraines and asthma were resolved through chiropractic care and a compassionate and understanding chiropractor mentored me to think positive thoughts and introduced the concept of Innate. All this resulted in choosing chiropractic as my profession.

As I sit here writing this book, the integration of Science and Spirit is gaining in popularity and so many of my questions are being answered. I'm sure there will always be more to learn, but at this point, Bruce Lipton's work has come closest in a scientific understanding of why believing in Innate reveals Wisdom.

Our genetic information is nothing more than physical memories of the organism's learned experiences. These learned experiences come from the reaction of the environment the cells have been forced to live in. When the environment becomes healthy, old cell memories are turned off and the cell then thrives. The bottom line is that "diseases are not the result of a single gene, but complex interactions among multiple genes and environmental factors" as so profoundly stated by Dr. Lipton in the aforementioned book.

There are two mechanisms that process the cell's information. We are taught that the genetic DNA is found in the nucleus of the cell. This is the natural mechanism in cell division. However, the latest research shows that enucleated cells (cells, which have had the nucleus removed) continue to thrive without genetic information for 2 to 3 months. Something other than genes continues to perform the functions of respiration, digestion, excretion and movement. This means that the DNA does not control cell function. The function of the DNA is to provide the cell's ability to reproduce and this is precisely the study of epigenetics. What is the control that is above genetics? There appears to be the nurturing mechanism of all cells that come from many sources, which include diet, exercise, positive thinking, prayer, meditation, practicing joy, peace, harmony and any ritual that elevates our conscious awareness that promotes homeostasis. In other words connecting with the cell's intelligent control that takes place in the absence of genes. This intelligence is found in the cell's membranes. Understanding the mechanisms that are controlled by the membrane translates environmental signals into behavior. This cellular behavior may be on a microscopic level, but what it has taught us is that behavior in a macroscopic level leads to harmony in community.

Science has given us an understanding of cellular biology. Philosophy has given us an understanding of the commonalities of belief systems. Cellular biology teaches us about the mechanics, which bring about the survival through an evolutionary process through the Innate Intelligence of the functioning membrane. Philosophy urges us to go deep into one's mind and pull out what resonates within us in order to live in a peaceful environment. At last, Science and Spirit are recognizing this integration more than ever in the 21st century. There are dozens of publications in this subject today that will challenge the minds of each and every one of us. Challenge yourself to have an open mind. Your own Innate Intelligence is definitely made from the image and likeness of the Universal Intelligence.

My own personal cancer healing experience of integrating body, mind and spirit cannot be discounted. Was it placebo? I hardly think so because the more we understand quantum physics and the tendency for something to be there or not be there, does challenge the black-and-white world of effects. Everything starts with an energy field, including our belief systems. The more you focus energy on any given set of circumstances, the greater the probability of manifesting this focus. Don't be misled that conventional research is the only way to advance. Be your own laboratory within yourself, because it is just as valid. There's an intercommunication that takes place when directing your own thoughts. It's up to you to communicate to yourself from that Innate level of understanding.

There will be many reading this book who are totally convinced of the need to use outside medical help. Protection and maintenance are both needed for survival of any organism, and I absolutely agree. Gaining an understanding of your own Intelligence within can help make choices that are fully congruent with your own belief systems. Belief in Innate does not mean turning away from other options; rather, it means intellectually approaching the problem with an open and receptive mind.

Growing in self-awareness creates an external environment to stimulate your cells to live in a harmonious cellular community and that translates to a healthier you.

I continue to marvel at the awesome effects of Innate taking place in the lives of my patients and in my own life. It never ceases to amaze me how Intelligent our Innate is. We cannot only use this Intelligence to help ourselves live healthier happier lives, but as we resonate this harmonious energy throughout our external environment as well, it can stir up a peaceful planet. I love the definition of "peace" from the *Random House Webster's College Dictionary* (1999): **1)** freedom from war, **2)** harmony among people, **3)** public order, **4)** freedom from anxiety, annoyance or mental disturbance, **5)** a state of tranquility or serenity, **6)** silence, **7)** to make peace with one's self, **8)** a way of saying farewell.

When asked why I did not write personal outcome stories, my response was ... no two stories can be identical. We all have our own narratives and results can only be evaluated by participating. Remember, I previously mentioned there is homework to do. This is a home study course. I would love to hear your experiences after you have worked the process. Send me your story through my website www.TreasuresFromMary.com or via snail mail to P.O. Box 231653, Encinitas CA 92023. With your permission I would love to tell your story in a future book.

Here are some patient comments after working the *Pick-of-the-Day* cards:

"I became empowered because I finally felt I could think for myself."

"There's still a lot of growing to do. I feel like I have a place to start now."

"I discovered I was leading my life through everyone's expectations of me."

"I learned that I need to take charge of my life."

"Doing these cards every day gave me permission to think things out for myself."

"The cards presented thoughts that hadn't occurred to me. I was just too busy."

"Wow! It stopped the poor-me attitude."

"The cards gave me a kick-start to be in a different awareness."

"Seeing my life change made me a believer."

"It helped me focus every day on self-improvement."

"It gave me more respect for myself and others."

"I didn't want to change anything, but down deep I knew I needed to. I just wasn't ready."

"I didn't give myself any credit until I really understood Innate. How come I was never taught that before?"

I assure you that the personal statements quoted by each person had profound life changing outcomes.

Realizing that we are body, mind and spirit is
the greatest gift we have, and merely knowing it is not enough.
This gift of realization has to be applied into a way of life.
It works when you work it, so work it!!!

PART II

PICK-OF-THE-DAY!

How to Use Part II

This section has been written as a companion to the *Pick-of-the-Day!* deck of cards. Keep the cards and book in a handy place, e.g. breakfast area, next to your favorite chair, your reading spot, or any location that is quiet. Find a place where your mornings begin. Shuffle the cards. Keep shuffling the cards until you feel satisfied with the vibration you receive from the top card. Then stop shuffling. Or, have your Daily Card electronically selected via the random card generator at my website. Read the card and the accompanied topic in **Part** II. To get the most benefit from each card and reading, do your best to *feel* what is being read and determine if you have an *emotion* that goes along with it. There are questions at the end of each section for reflection and introspection. See what you have attracted as the activity. No, this is not fortune telling. The attraction is what your Innate is presenting to your own investigative laboratory. (That laboratory is...your own life!) During the day actively participate in its message to the best of your understanding and perspective. Make sure you return the card to the deck. Continue this process for one month and keep a tally of what cards came up for you on a recurrent basis. Don't be surprised if you end up drawing the same cards fairly often. Focus on the first four topics most repeated. These may be areas that need your continued attention. Innate will guide you. Remember, life is like a game and it's all about how you Innately play it!

See **Appendix A** for an example of a record-keeping chart.
Note: If you make your own cards, I recommend the entire deck be made before you start the tally process.

The following is an example of a case history:
The patient fully embodied Innate within and believed and accepted that this concept was the guidance needed when drawing the shuffled cards. A record was kept for three consecutive months. The results below only show the cards that were selected with the first four highest topic repeats.

Results of the first month:
1) Open Your Eyes (selected 7 times during the month)
2) Trust (selected 6 times during the month)
3) Courage (selected 4 times during the month)
4) Peace card and Food for Thought card (each were selected three times during the month)

Results of the second month:
1) Open your Eyes (selected 7 times during the month)
2) Intuition (selected 6 times during the month)
3) Peace (selected 3 times during the month)
4) Gratefulness (selected 3 times during the month)

Results of the third month:
1) Peace (selected 7 times during the month)
2) Open Your Eyes (selected 4 times during the month)
3) Kindness (selected 4 times during the month)
4) Life is like a game (selected 4 times during the month)

At the end of the three months using the cards, the similarities that came up were re-evaluated. During the interview, this patient's case history presented a picture of what was revealed about his outlook in life.

The results were accepted with an open mind. The patient realized that appearances cannot be judged because there is always more than what meets the eye. This generated a kinder attitude towards people no matter who they were. He began to trust himself more often realizing that intuitive feelings had value, which brought about more inner peace. An attitude of gratefulness brought about more contentment. The final outcome of learning to participate more fully in life resulted in a more harmonious family and also the accompanying adverse physical conditions that were being experienced had been markedly reduced. The patient continued to use the cards regularly and has since made up a few new ones that pertain to his own self-improvement issues.

Author's note: I realize that not everyone will follow through with the suggestions for using the cards or completely embody the Innate concept. The aforementioned case history presented was exceptional and what were the odds that someone would have this result? To draw the "Open Your Eyes" card 18 times in three months was truly an "eye opener" (no pun intended) to both the patient and myself. This particular patient had the perseverance to follow suggestions for using the cards and participate to the fullest. The results were well beyond mere chance and not everyone had the startling results this case history presented. Other patient results were fragmented, but they all still derived enlightenment from use of the cards. Experiment for yourself and see what happens. Everyone's results will be different; just do your best to embody Innate when shuffling and drawing your cards.

In my own personal experience, the cards were written about a year before deciding to write this book. I shuffled the cards and picked a card to write about. It was the card on "Priorities". After writing on this topic, I returned the "Priorities" card back to the deck. The very next time I sat down to write about a different card, shuffled them, and out came the "Priorities" card again. Talking to myself, I said, "I just wrote on that one." So, I shuffled again. The same card was selected 4 times in a row. Then my immediate thoughts were…this must be telling me something. I'll never get this book written if I keep pulling the same card. I removed the "Priorities" card from the deck, proceeded to draw another card, and got "Life is like a game". It happened 3 days in a row – same card! It really got me thinking. What is this telling me? So, I removed that card as well from the deck. As the days went by I made sure the cards were together to avoid any misplacement and returned the 2 removed cards back to the deck. When I became motivated to write again, shuffled the cards, and sure enough the "Priorities" card was drawn again. I got the message and thought to myself…What were the odds from drawing the same cards again? Could this be the Law of Attraction at work? I believe there is a Law of Attraction, but somehow when it actually happens it is often thought of as a "red flag" or a "good hunch". Once again, removing the "Priorities" card, I drew again. You guessed it! "Life is like a game". There was the realization that my motivation to write this book was presenting itself as a priority. My patients have long encouraged me to write because I have often referred to "life is like a game". We manifest our beliefs and habits. Our life and our health reflect our thoughts.

    I am grateful now that I made the effort to put this book into print. I encourage you to see how your own Innate will guide you because Innate is the best friend you have! Have a great day!

With love, Dr. Mary

Recognize and claim your Innate Intelligence.
It can never be separated from Universal Intelligence.
Therein lies your power!

> **Open Your Eyes**
>
> *See each day with a new awareness.*
> *Restore your capacity to*
> *see beyond appearances.*

Are you in a rut doing the same thing or thinking the same way? Either you are content with the way life is going or change is needed. Change doesn't have to be a "pick-up" and move type of thing. It can take place exactly where you are. In other words, find a new way of looking at yourself by how you view the persons, places, things, circumstances, relationships, money or whatever is around you. Is there anything that preoccupies your mind creating a barrier? See beyond appearances. Dare to be creative.

I can remember as a child that my mother would rearrange the furniture in the living room to stir up a change. Just that little bit of creativity brought us to enthusiastic gatherings in the sitting room of our small living quarters. The whole family wanted to feel the change. Being creatures of habit, the boredom returned again after a period of time. We tend to fall back to what is familiar even if it's not particularly suitable anymore.

Opening your eyes to a new awareness can restore your capacity to see beyond appearances. Albert Einstein once said, "No problem can be solved from the same consciousness that created it."

Maybe it's time to take inventory! The inventory of your thoughts and the feelings that generate from the reflection of what you see.

Let's start with small things. Yes, even small things can have a legacy. What kind of legacy are you creating? What is it that you want to leave behind to be remembered? Step aside for a few moments to look at your life. Open your eyes to observe the person that you are. What do you see? It's OK to be truthful with yourself because only you have to know about your inner thoughts.

Make a list of the things you like and don't like about yourself. There are many opportunities to refine your life beyond appearances. The mere fact that you recognized the need for change is an admirable quality.

This topic starts **Part II** of this book and later when you select the *Open Your Eyes* card, see yourself from the place of an observer. That's right, step outside of yourself. The ego has many appearances, but the real you underneath of all the coverings and dressings is what contains the invisible eyes that can see beyond appearances. I challenge you to resonate with all the love and creativity that is your birthright. It's that part of you that belongs only to you and it's there just by opening your eyes.

Questions

1. Are there parts of you difficult to see?

2. Is there something that tells you that you may not be capable of this inner vision?

3. Are you willing to make a list of who you are and create your legacy?

> **Criticism**
>
> *Today, think before you speak about others. Are your comments meant to hurt or heal?*

Most of us talk all day long no matter where we are, whether it's at work, home, school, fun or just relaxing. My challenge to you today is to mentally keep track of conversations that end up revolving around other people. I know this may be a hard assignment. Do the best you can. When we talk, we generally use a lot of descriptive phrases, e.g. he or she is a nice person, or delightful, pretty, intelligent, lovely, etc. He or she is a mean person, or stupid, obnoxious, jerk, etc. I'm sure you get the idea. Sometimes we talk in this manner not even realizing what is said. However, if you hear another person talk about someone else with positive or negative connotations, it may stir up thoughts of judgment. Depending on the nature of the conversation or the comments, think about the intention. Are the comments meant to hurt or heal? Sometimes as a result of our own frustrations, we casually put down another person. Sometimes we are enamored by someone and those comments can fill us with a sense of respect or admiration.

When I was very young, I often heard this phrase, "If you can't say something nice about someone, don't say it at all." Have you heard the same phrase?

One of the things I've learned through treating patients and myself included, is that the better I feel physically and mentally, I see other people the same way. It has opened my eyes that the best way to overcome criticism is to work on your own self worth. Work on your own health in order to have the energy needed to meet each day. A balanced life allows you to see things more clearly and have a perspective of what it means to develop a positive outlook.

It seems like what it all boils down to is trust. Our conversations with others create a trust. No matter what the situation, if you speak highly of someone, it becomes a reassurance this person will speak highly of you when you're not present. Where and how do you want your gossip to go? Let's face it. We all gossip.

When the *Criticism* card is picked, think in terms of the Golden Rule – do unto others as you would have them do unto you. All cultures and civilizations have innately adopted this universal principle. In so doing, the law of attraction that applies to physics also applies to our lives in relationship, business, friends, etc. It all starts with an awareness of the spoken word.

Questions

1. Are you up for the challenge of being aware of how you speak about others? It's probably one of the hardest tasks we can meet in our daily lives.

2. How do you interpret how others see you? Are you part of the problem or part of the solution?

3. Do you get offended easily? If so, it may be a sign there is inner work to do. Remember, we cannot separate the body/mind connection. Observe your body's signs and see what feeling and emotion comes up during those times you may feel offended.

> **Look for the Good**
>
> *Today, look for the good in someone.*
> *As you recognize the good,*
> *it is also a part of you.*

Have you ever fallen into a cycle that no matter what's going on, there is always someone who seems to "push your buttons"? Every day in practice patients tell me stories about spouses, parents, children, bosses and/or co-workers that "push buttons". What I find interesting is that I rarely hear anything contrary about their dog or cat. A dog said to his master, "You are god. You feed me." A cat said to his master, "I must be a god, because you feed me." The dog recognizes the good. The cat has already recognized the good in self. Both attributes are equally important.

When we recognize the good in someone, are we not recognizing that part of ourselves? Otherwise how else could we be recognizing it? It's like looking into a mirror. What you are looking at, you are looking with!

Physical symptoms often correlate with how we view ourselves, others and/or circumstances. An example would be describing lower back pain and complaining about someone or something as being a "pain in the butt". There is a connection between the body and mind. Observe yourself and take a mental test regarding your own symptoms and what you may be thinking. Do this exercise often. It takes time to figure out this connection, just like Rome wasn't built in a day.

For many it will take a mental lifestyle change. For others, it may be already part of who they are. The more you recognize the good in others, the more you see those aspects of yourself becoming clearer.

The place to start is with the very next person you encounter. Don't be discouraged if you can't master this task all at once. Believe me, there will be lots of opportunities every day. Be assertive with yourself and do not let one slip by.

Remember that life is like a game and it's how you Innately play it. There are no other opponents because the only real player is yourself in the way you act or react.

I challenge you to be more aware of how you look at yourself and others as you step into this new world that awaits. As it unfolds, you will be amazed at how everyone seems to have changed for the better around you. Did I really say that? It's really a paradox. As you change your way of looking at things, seeing the good in others changes your perspective.

The dog looks to his master with an openness and receptivity. The cat, on the other hand, appears self-centered, but as we recognize these attributes within, where does it all come from? I like to believe that these good qualities come from our Master Creator that has gifted us with an Intelligence far beyond what words can articulate. You have to answer that question yourself. Where does it come from?

Questions

1. Are you guilty of wanting to change others, but not yourself?

2. Are you willing to look into the mirror and see your reflection with a new set of eyes?

3. If this is a difficult task, ask yourself, "Do I need a dog?" Dogs have such unconditional love. Dog owners will tell you that over and over again. Ok, if you want to, pick a cat.

Patience

Learning to be patient helps you to understand self. Impatience can be an aspect of causing distress to others and self. Think before you speak.

What kind of situations are you experiencing when being impatient? Is it health related, family stress, career doubt or challenges, lack of self-motivation, expressed or repressed anger? Only you can identify and feel any discomfort within yourself. Think about what might be causing the impatience?

Does your life revolve around instant gratification? So much advertising leaves us with a subliminal message that with a click of your fingers, it should all happen. Even computers are faster than ever before. Faster doesn't mean it's bad even though there are many advantages to quick and instant results. What I'm talking about here is "old fashion" patience. The patience that can come from character building, understanding one's self and the ability to imagine walking in another person's shoes.

Patience can also come from an understanding of a deeper resource than the outside world. It can come from believing there's an inner guidance that resonates with evidence that all things manifest in a timely manner and are expressed and experienced as running smoothly. Even more love expressing in your life can be a reflection of inner and outer patience.

Have you ever tried to force things to happen because of impatience? What percentages of the outcomes were actually favorable and were without stress? There are some that will say that if they didn't act immediately they would have lost out. That's true and I can attest to that myself. In those cases, I like to think that the time was right for the opportunity.

Many mistakes can happen when there is impatience, like saying the wrong thing without thinking. Was it because a defense mechanism came into play and it felt justified at the time? However, if the damaging response was left unsaid, the end result might have been different.

I've had patients tell me that this happens in families and they became estranged. Looking back over past events, much of it came as a result of being impatient with the actions and decisions of others. Patience takes practice. It develops into knowing when to act and when not to act. It's our reaction to things without thinking first, that accompanies impatience.

When the *Patience* card is selected, take a deep breath. Think to yourself. "What's my hurry in this very moment?" Depending on the circumstances, allow yourself a moment, a few seconds, an hour, a day, a week, a month, a year, or whatever the situation warrants. Each person can evaluate this application to his or her present decision-making process, whether it is in a conversation or purchasing a major item. Know the differences between the responses of short and long-term patience. With this understanding of self-patience, you will become more understanding of others. Patience, however, is not a pass-card to justify procrastination.

Questions

1. If you are an impatient person, can you catch yourself when it happens? What's the subject at hand?

2. Is impatience with yourself, others or both?

3. After you have recognized when you are patient or impatient, how does it make you feel? Was there an emotion that goes with it? Were you able to think first or did the response come from a habit?

Light

Today, brighten your inner light by being more radiant in your smiles.

I don't think there is any one person who would not prefer to be lighter. I'm not talking about physical weight. I'm talking about cheerfulness that can lighten and elevate our disposition. We all have the ability and the power to lighten up our lives, not only by our thinking, but also with an outward expression. Are you in the habit of smiling a lot or do you constantly wear a frown? I've had patients tell me, there's not much to smile about because of one reason or another. Changing your mind or your outlook on things isn't easy in certain situations. That's understandable. If that's the case, maybe it's time to lighten up. A place to start may be out in the public where no one knows what you carry within your inner self. Giving a smile to someone and watching a return smile can be lots of fun because it doesn't make any difference what background, belief system, nationality or culture is involved. A smile is a smile all over the planet. It's a way of communicating with someone without a spoken word. In fact, it may be just what the doctor ordered to help lighten one's moment or day. It may even be your own day, especially if you are not in the habit of smiling.

The next time you're out in a store, or for a walk, or traveling, watch the faces of the people around you. Focus your attention on how others around you relate to one another. Experiment with the idea. Smile at someone and see what happens. Do they smile back? Do you get ignored? If at all possible, see if the feedback from the other person causes them to look at a different stranger in a more cheerful way as a result of the smile that you gave them.

Politeness with a smile can be contagious.

Practice going around with a smile on your face. Others may wonder what you are up to. I have had people say to me, "What's going on? You're really smiling! What's funny?" Others will often want to get into that space with you.

Lighting up your life with radiant smiles can lighten up another person's life as well. If we could all make an effort to show that cheerfulness by smiling, it may make a difference in not only your own world, but also in someone else's.

When you select the *Light* card, think about how frequently you wear a smile. It takes 17 muscles to smile, and 43 muscles to frown. Just think of the amount of consumed muscle contraction energy it takes to frown, and not only that, it may cause wrinkles on your face. With so many people being conscious of beauty tips, what better way to look beautiful than to sparkle with a radiant smile.

Questions

1. Are you willing to try the experiment?

2. If you're not used to smiling, then go look at yourself in a mirror. See the face you carry around with you. If you do smile a lot, still look in the mirror.

3. Are you taking life too seriously that you forgot how to be cheerful? Think about it.

> **Food for Thought**
>
> *You are part of the inter-connectedness of the Universe by virtue of your consciousness. What you say makes a difference.*

This *Pick-of-the-Day!* card doesn't necessarily have any special activity associated with it, unless, "food for thought" requires effort. Otherwise, let it flow naturally. That, you will see, is an activity in itself.

We are all inter-connected to the vastness of all there is, just by being. What we say and what we feel can make a difference in our perception of this inter-connectedness. Whether we realize it or not, the inner-connectedness (another way of saying how Innate is connected with the Self) expands into the inter-connectedness throughout the universe. It's only our thinking and state of consciousness that gives us the experience of how we interpret life.

There are numerous books written about the power of positive thinking and what happens in our life as a result of its applications. Our thinking and attitudes can cascade into a fulfilling life whether we lead a simple lifestyle in a small cottage or apartment or to the magnitude of giving and receiving as demonstrated by Oprah Winfrey.

Writing this book and working with the deck of cards has emphasized a greater awareness of my inner-connectedness of the Self and how it has an inter-connectedness with the Universe.

There's an expression that goes something like this: "it works, if you work it, so work it."

As you ponder on your own life at this particular time, how does inter-connectedness via your inner-connectedness look to you? Is it weaving a beautiful tapestry as you fill in life's events? Or, does your personal tapestry need to be refined from this day forward? Is it time to create the masterpiece? Remember, we are made from the same particles as the stars. "We have a right to be here" as I reflect those words from the *Desiderata*. We can shine our inner light and what we say does make a difference.

As we go forth this day, see yourself connected to everything else. We live in an era when an idea or thought is but a keystroke away. The Internet has expanded communication to all parts of the globe. Messages sent back to Earth from the Pioneer 10 spacecraft in 1972 allowed us to better comprehend the huge scope of this inter-connectedness. I like to think that we have the same ability to send a deep message into our inner space and the space of our neighbor by just being and knowing our consciousness connects everything.

Visualization has also helped many people heal their own physical bodies by inner-connecting with the Innate Intelligence within. There's a Wisdom that we may not fully understand, but seeing it as perfect, complete and whole can remove barriers.

The *Food for Thought* card challenges you to expand your personal perception of consciousness to include all there is. If that's too difficult, take only one object, such as a flower, a paper clip, a pencil, or just any object. In your mind, break the object down into the fine particles it is made of and then into the energy field that holds it together and know that you are there by virtue of your consciousness.

Questions

1. How deep can you go within your consciousness?

2. Are you limiting your field of perception? If so, why?

3. After you have "worked it", what differences do you see within yourself that it works? Changes won't happen overnight. It takes practice, but "it does work".

Evenness

There may be ups and downs, but learning to adapt by quieting the mind, allows you to learn acceptance and detach from outcomes.

How many times a day does your mind respond like a yo-yo? As a child, playing with other children, we trained ourselves to make the yo-yo sleep. It took practice. It's the same way it is with the ups and downs of our lives. It takes practice to remain "even" and to quiet the mind, and not over-react to challenging circumstances that come our way.

Do you feel a need to control all things? Take a look at our own body mechanisms. Within your own body, you have both voluntary and involuntary actions. The involuntary actions are working without conscious direction. We don't have to direct our heart to beat. It does that automatically. The voluntary actions can be controlled, like lifting your arms or walking from one spot to another. It's easy to see the difference. However, we can voluntarily quiet our mind and our heartbeat can slow down, but it doesn't just stop! The opposite is also true. We can get emotional over something and our heart will race. Our reaction to events can be like the yo-yo. Learning to quiet our reactions, to think, to be aware, and to prepare ourselves in the best way enables us to be ready for the challenges we face. Outcomes may not always be the way we want them, but by quieting the mind we can be open to options and therefore, become unattached to every outcome. To think that life is always about perfect outcomes is unrealistic. This teaches us acceptance.

The serenity prayer takes on a whole new meaning when we learn to be "even".

"God grant me the serenity to accept the things I cannot change, courage to change the things I can, and the wisdom to know the difference."

Even though we have the gift to change our lives, being able to quiet our minds and enter into that space between the thought and the response takes discipline. Therein lies your power. Evenness is an asset in identifying inner Wisdom. Decisions to either accept and/or control outcomes will have more clarity.

How does it feel when you are in that space of evenness, regardless of outcomes? Does it make you feel helpless or a master of your own thoughts? Does your heart rate go up or down? Have you learned to do the tricks that are hidden within the yo-yo?

When you select the *Evenness* card and events are like a roller coaster in your life, mentally picture the sleeping yo-yo. Become skillful at quieting the mind, if only for a brief second. Take a deep breath and observe how you feel.

Questions

1. Are you a victim of the responses to these ups and downs in your life? Do you act or react?

2. Are you willing to stop the chatter in your mind for a brief moment to detach from the outcomes of distracted thoughts?

3. Can you accept that not all things are under your control?

Control

Today, admit to yourself that you do not always know what is best. This is why one turns to prayer or introspection for Higher Wisdom.

Turning to prayer can often mean different things to different people. Some prayers seem to be a begging or a beseeching process, and other prayers are for an openness to be receptive to insights for introspection that might provide help and guidance.

There are times when I just can't figure out what is best for me, but I know the answers can be obtained from somewhere. Sometimes the answers don't come right away, and when that happens, the situation makes me feel a lack of control. The more I communicate with others about this, the more I find it's a common scenario.

What works for me may not necessarily work for you. Cookbook approaches may only serve as a place to start and must be modified as more and more becomes revealed. Turning to a Higher Wisdom can come in many forms.

I like to capitalize the words "Higher Wisdom" because it denotes a Wisdom that is more than I can completely understand. There is always more to learn about what helps us to grow and mature. Being able to admit that we do not know everything and are not always in control keeps us humble. Someone once told me, "We must let our nothingness get out of the way to make room for the Divine". Is this not the same as seeking that Higher Wisdom?

On the flip side, having control is also an asset. Being able to control our minds to go into the silent part of us to wait for insights to be revealed may be the most powerful tool we have. It allows our Higher Wisdom to reveal answers when we consciously may not know what is best.

Don't take my word for it! Do it for yourself. Trust this Higher Wisdom and when you have repeatedly demonstrated the outcomes from this introspection, you will have discovered the secret that lies in the very depths of who you are. A knowingness will come that only you can interpret. Why? Because the answers will be clear to you and no one else will see it from your perspective.

When you select the *Control* card, turn towards your inner Higher Wisdom for insights. Prayer is just another word for being focused on that part of you that connects with a Higher Intelligence. If at first you don't succeed, try and try again. It works!

Questions

1. What do you think of when you hear the words "prayer" and/or "Higher Wisdom"? You have the choice; it can be anything you want it to be.

2. If the words "prayer" and/or "Higher Wisdom" don't work for you, replace them with words you are comfortable with to search for your own answers. Maybe "God" works better for you. Words are only man-made descriptions formed in a language to help each other communicate. The perceptions inside of you are what really count.

3. Ask yourself if it's necessary to surrender to this "Higher Wisdom". If not, why not?

> **Gratefulness**
>
> *Say 10 things you are grateful for three times a day!*

In medicine, therapeutic doses are often given every 4-6 hours. Allow this card to be personal therapeutic dose that keeps you in a state of gratitude throughout the day.

To get started in the beginning say anything that comes to mind that expresses gratefulness - family, job, health, etc.

To get more specific in our gratefulness expressions there are five basic life categories:

1. spiritual
2. mental
3. physical
4. social/relationship
5. prosperity

As each category is dissected, it will help you get deeper into learning what it is like to have a positive attitude towards yourself and others.

If this task is harder than it appears, make a mental note of what happened in this process. Did you get hung-up on certain aspects? If so, just that awareness is empowering. Empowerment is recognizing that we have choices. Having a perspective that leads to fulfilling choices increases our grateful attitude towards life.

The spiritual category focuses on what that means to you? Examine what it means to be spiritual and/or religious? One can be spiritual without religion and vice versa; however, you can be both. What are you grateful for?

The mental category revolves around what flows in and out of your mind. Are there challenges that keep repeating themselves? Or, have you mastered positive reactions to various challenges? What are you grateful for?

The physical category is directed towards health, exercise, diet, and/or general physical well-being. This part of life gets a lot of attention, but it also has mixed messages, and the messages keep changing. Years ago it was OK to smoke cigarettes, but now even second hand smoke is labeled as a "killer". Advertisements urge you to ask the doctor, "Is this [drug] right for me?" There are benefits to both conventional and alternative approaches to physical well being. Be grateful we are part of the information age and able to make wise choices. Most of all look to what feels intuitively right for you. What are you grateful for?

The social/relationship category seems to include story after story of dysfunctional lifestyles, slander, illegal activities, or a plethora of undesired behaviors. The media seem to prefer telling stories about the negative aspects of our society. Is it because positive stories do not draw viewer attention? Do our priorities about life need to be re-examined? What are you grateful for?

The last category, prosperity, usually centers on money, success and net worth. Prosperity means different things to different people. I like to think of prosperity as abundance, and that abundance can show up in all parts of life. One question to ask yourself is, "Am I truly content with my prosperity or am I just fooling myself? Is your answer an excuse for lack of focus, direction or motivation? What are you grateful for?

Verbalizing 10 statements of gratitude may be very easy for some because they are areas taken for granted. But, I'm asking you to re-think your inventory with feelings of gratefulness. Being grateful needs to come from a place of knowing and experiencing that gratefulness. In turn, it may be the same list, but adding the feeling dissipates what is taken for granted.

When you select the *Gratefulness* card, I challenge you to feel that gratefulness well up from within. If you find it difficult to create the list, work diligently on owning the feeling and the emotion that goes with it, it's something that can change your life.

Questions

1. How easy was it to verbalize 10 things you are grateful for?

2. How easy was it to pick a category? How easy was it to digest what each category was all about?

3. Are you taking your inventory for granted? Or, do you have a new appreciation of how you are living your life?

> **Habits**
>
> *It takes 21 to 30 days to form a habit. Start today to make positive changes in your life.*

Many years ago I read in a book that it takes 21 days to form a habit. It's been my experience that it takes longer for some people. I figured what harm would it do to just try it out? Amazingly enough, it works! It's a surefire way to create both good habits and, unfortunately, bad habits as well.

Take the time to reflect on changes that you would like to make in your life. Don't just think about them; make a written list. The list may include simple things as making your bed every morning or putting your keys in a special location so that they don't get misplaced. It doesn't have to be complex. The list might also include telling someone you love him or her more often.

Changes don't happen overnight for the most part. Turn the process into a game. It's not necessary to work on every item on your list all at once. The most important factor is to be consistent with actions and before you know it, it will turn into a natural way of doing things. It's actually fun. Soon you'll stop thinking about the habit you want to establish or accomplish because it will already be automatic.

Maybe you want to include exercise, reading, meditating, or something else you don't seem to make time for. Schedule it into your activities, and before long those appointments you make with yourself will turn into habits.

Be reasonable when making the list. Don't defeat yourself before starting the process. The whole idea is to make life easier. When routine daily things run more smoothly unexpected situations can be handled more efficiently and more effectively.

Form a habit to select a *Pick-of-the-Day!* card each day. Doing so may be the impetus that is needed to work on self-improvement. Daily introspection can also be habit forming.

When you select the *Habits* card remind yourself of the fun it can be to make changes in this game called "Life". You are the main character. Be responsible and learn to make wise choices.

Questions

1. Do you really want to make new habits to change your life, or are you happy with everything you do?

2. Is your mind telling you to put off starting the 21 to 30 day approach until later, or are you willing to start now?

3. If the answer is to start later, what's stopping you from starting now? Think about it. Is your reason a good one, or are you procrastinating.

Attitude

Attitudes can make or break a person. What's your attitude been like lately? Do you need to cultivate a new way of seeing or doing things? Hmmm…

Everyone innately knows when their attitude gets in the way of progress. Some people are so fixed in their attitudes that they fail to look at anyone else's point of view. Being open and receptive in your attitude are more than just being open and receptive. It takes understanding. For example, let's take two separate views of the same thing: yours and someone else's. Each is convinced they cannot compromise their views. A new way of looking at things might be to fully understand the other's point of view and having the other person understand your point of view. Outcomes can be either a mutual compromise, or maybe a whole new way of looking at the situation that incorporates each other's attitudes…thus, finding the best of both worlds.

The attitude challenge may be in the way you handle personal views on diet, exercise, work, recreation, worship, personal growth, and/or lifestyle. Do you have any hang ups that haunt you daily? It may be time to give the attitude role a closer look. A change in attitude can either make or break you. Giving up an undesirable or bad attitude takes hard work, just like adopting a new attitude. Are you up for a new outlook? Or, does it seem too hard to make changes in your life?

Think of change as a game, and make it a game with only win-win situations. Don't make the game so difficult that you may feel defeated before you even start.

Get personal with yourself. The answers are for yourself, not for anyone else. What's your attitude been like lately? Are your attitudes cyclical? Can you catch yourself when attitudes begin to change? What does it feel like? How does your emotion fit into it? Can you feel yourself going downhill prior to an attitude shift? Can you feel yourself perk-up when things feel right?

Being an observer of changing moods can be a key to progress. Pay attention to what causes your moods and attitudes to change. It could be related to the foods you eat, or the amount of rest you are getting or whether you are burning the candle at both ends. It may even be the need to be kinder to yourself and others. All of these situations take understanding.

When you select the *Attitude* card, ponder on how you perceive and understand the circumstances at hand. Don't be just open and receptive; be open and receptive *with understanding*. Think of how much you can learn.

Questions

1. Are you a victim of your attitude fluctuations?

2. Are you willing to seek a better understanding before making decisions?

3. Does your attitude need to get better or are you already perfect? Hmmm…

Responsibility

*Wake up to responsibility.
Ignoring it doesn't make it go away.
Turn your responsibility into a
gift for self-growth.*

Sometimes undesirable circumstances in our life materialize before we've even had time to think about them. Actions take place before the awareness becomes evident. This could allow one to become a victim of circumstances. Waking up to awareness helps in making wise choices. Ignoring signs of accountability can get you into trouble.

What are the circumstances in your life right now that are in need of repair? Do they involve health issues, relationship, finances, career, retirement, addiction? What would be different had you acted more responsibly? Don't beat yourself up anymore over the past, because "today is the first day of the rest of your life". Those words have saved the day for me and countless others. Its value, when taken to heart, can be the motive to become responsible from now on. A doctor friend once said to me, "Then is then, and now is now". How right he was! The present is all we really have, so start with where you are. Make each moment a gift to do what needs to be done to improve any situation you are facing. Wake up to responsibility for your own thoughts, actions and activities. Take action steps rather than having lingering thoughts of the past.

If you are already a responsible person, ask what awareness qualities contributed to this attribute? How were they developed?

Each of us has an inner voice that tells us what direction we need to follow. Is the conversation you have with that inner voice resonating to right purpose, right action, and right effort? Taking action steps to be responsible and accountable manifests in right understanding.

Decision-making based on right understanding results in a feeling of being "in the flow of life". It doesn't mean everything will be smooth sailing, but the valued gift that comes with responsible awareness produces stability.

When the *Responsibility* card is selected, see yourself as a vibrant person full of life's gifts. Being responsible isn't a burden. Burdens result from a lack of right action and/or right effort. Set your thinking straight.

Questions

1. What does responsibility mean to you?

2. Are you willing to be accountable for your own outcomes? If not, why? Are you blaming others?

3. Are you aware that life is all about choices? Choose wisely to make it a gift rather than a burden.

Awareness

Today, observe any signs that cause distress. Accept them as an opportunity to create a win-win-situation.

Visualize yourself driving a car and it approaches a traffic light. The light turns red and you stop. While waiting for the light to turn green, do you take the opportunity to see what's around you? Are other drivers calm or distracted? Are they paying attention or talking on their cell phones? Are cars crowding in to get around the corner as soon as possible? Are there pedestrians waiting to cross? Are there signs and shrubbery blocking your view of oncoming traffic? Being observant gives you an edge on how to proceed. You may also have expanded your awareness by looking at other makes and colors of cars, stores in the neighborhood, checking out directions, or any number of things. We observe a lot of information in a brief period of time.

What would happen if you weren't paying attention? Things would be less likely to work out as planned. You might not see the light change until the last minute, causing you to slam on your brakes. You might miss the corner where you were supposed to turn, causing you to be late for an important date. The resulting stress might make you feel as if you'd been thrown into a lose-lose situation, thereby seeing yourself as a "victim" of circumstance.

Immediately prior to any unfavorable circumstance, what did your mind tell you? Was there a small still voice speaking within that could have helped you be more aware? Were intuitive signs ignored that preceded the outcome? Did you miss the opportunity?

Do you make it a habit of missing opportunities? Awareness comes from being alert to each moment and being in the present time. The next time you feel like a "victim" of unfavorable circumstances, employ a bit of hindsight: Ask yourself what was learned from this event and how it could have turned into a win-win situation?

The analogy of driving a car is simple, but it's a good reminder that you are in the driver's seat. Of course, there will always be unexpected challenges, but you can be better prepared for them by being aware. Training the mind to be aware is like having a precognitive sense. Be your own psychic without having to make an appointment with a "reader" to see into the future.

Sharpening awareness takes practice. The more practice, the more aware you will become. You will be surprised at how, with continued awareness, the very thing you need will miraculously appear.

I've heard so many people say to me, "All I was doing was thinking about something or someone, and suddenly the information or person just showed up." After a while, when this is practiced often enough, it becomes a way of life. The awareness you are seeking is also seeking you.

The next time awareness presents itself, and your thoughts get processed in your mind, what happened next? Certainty or doubt? I've heard myself and others say, "I knew it. I just knew it!" One may wonder if their thoughts created the outcome, or was it just a lack of observation.

It reminds me of the search for Schrodinger's Cat in particle physics. In this scientific experiment, the outcome of what happens to a particle is only revealed when it becomes observed. Searching for reality sometimes seems fruitless, but as we continue to search for this awareness, it can lead us to a new understanding of reality.

When the *Awareness* card is selected, I challenge you to use your awareness to transform your day and to transcend your thinking into a win-win situation. Don't be trapped into a conventional interpretation of the why's and how's something should not work. Don't beat yourself up by thinking you may lose. Change your thinking. Change your life.

Questions

1. Are you too busy to take the time to be more aware?

2. Are you so overwhelmed by outside distractions that your responses are coming from memory programming?

3. Are you willing to accept the consequences of unawareness? (Awareness also has consequences, but somehow Innate helps us not feel like a "victim" of circumstances.)

> **Be Receptive**
>
> *Every day is a new day.*
> *See something new*
> *in your everyday world.*
> *Make simple things an adventure.*

Being receptive reminds me of the phrase, "stop and smell the roses". The whole world around us contains vast amounts of so-called "miracles", and so many new things to explore. Pause here for a moment, and ask yourself what immediately came to mind as something new that you were exposed to recently? Whatever it was, shrink yourself down to its level and become an adventurer. See where it takes you. How does it feel to explore this new world? What emotion can you identify with in this new place? What can you learn from this adventure?

When visiting an unfamiliar place, sometimes the journey does not always turn out as expected. Some examples could be: watching a tiny insect crawling across a leaf to get to a flower of magnificent color; envisioning a red blood cell traveling through the narrow straits of a capillary; walking through a botanical garden and seeing the unusual blooms we never knew existed. Each experience creates new outlooks.

Close your eyes for just a few moments. Empty your thoughts, if you can. With your eyes still closed, scan the room with your mind. Find a place where scanning stops. As you open your eyes, what is directly in front of them? For that moment, create a new adventure. Take a few moments to investigate the first object your eyes fall upon. If it was a book on the shelf, for example, go to the book and open it to a random page. What does it say? What can you learn from this exercise?

Many times our world is so busy that we don't stop to "smell the roses". If you can identify with this lifestyle and there isn't enough time in the day for everything, then you need this exercise more than you may think. It only takes a few moments. The benefits can be most rewarding. It can calm you in the midst of a "rat race" or personal turmoil. It's a brief way of getting outside a situation and being receptive to many new things you never knew existed. It can clear your mind so that when you return, the visions or views are clearer and more enhanced. Now return to the everyday world with a fresh look.

There is much to see and be part of in the outside world. Expand your horizons. Make life an adventure. You'll be glad you did.

Make it a habit to *Be Receptive,* not just today, but every day.

Questions

1. Did your adventure to a new place tell you anything about your inner Self?

2. Did your adventure open up a new interest that you want to learn more about?

3. Did your adventure make you realize how often you need to "stop to smell the roses"?

Growing Pains

*Each adverse situation you encounter is
an opportunity for growth.
Recognize the obstacle.
The real enemy
might be a negative reaction.*

Have you ever found yourself saying, "I'm tired of all this crap?" Growing pains are the frustrations that keep repeating over and over again.

Einstein once said that you can't change something with the same consciousness that created it. It may be time to observe yourself. Creating a win-win situation takes one out of a selfish position to one in which everyone wins.

The battle of who is winning may actually be within yourself. The players may be your small still voice and your knee jerk reaction.

Have you ever caught yourself answering questions with the same introductory words such as "no...", or "yes, but..."? These words may be enemies in disguise.

Or, there might be a different scenario that triggers an obstacle. Maybe just reading this for the first time is causing a knee jerk reaction that's putting up a barrier in your mind. Once again, be the observer. Is your reaction the real enemy?

Recognizing that you are becoming tired of those growing pains is a great place to start in the process of personal growth.

Admitting to yourself that something may not be working in your life is an opportunity to make different choices.

If things are already working, does that mean choices are in the right direction? Life is always about choice. No matter what the circumstances, the common denominator is personal choice. We may not always be able to pick ourselves up and physically move away from situations; however, our reactions and attitudes can bring about significant changes.

What are your feelings when something "rubs you the wrong way"? Is there an emotion that goes with it? Are you "passing the buck" and blaming someone or something else for your reaction? "Change your thinking, change your life!" That expression has been around for a long time. Transform "growing pains" into "growing".

When you select the *Growing Pains* card, ask yourself if you have made progress in that department. Find ways to catch yourself in reactive patterns that need to be addressed.

If you don't want to grow, then don't do anything about it. Enjoy anger, fear, jealousy, persecution, etc. When you get tired of the same "crap", then the time is right to release the growing pains.

Questions

1. Do you like your personality when you are on the defensive?

2. Have you tasted what harmony in yourself and relationships are like?

3. On a scale of 1 to 10 where does your "growing pains" fit in? (The higher the number the more you are experiencing growing pains)
1...2...3...4...5...6...7...8...9...10
(Mentally circle a number.)

Courage

*It takes courage to be confronted.
Develop and practice inner strength.
It's a source of courage.*

Some people feel the need for courage in meeting life's challenges. Obstacles may appear as big as mountains, and overcoming the journey's challenges takes courage.

Some people have consequences to face and are afraid. That takes courage. Even admitting mistakes takes a certain amount of courage.

Maybe courage is needed in facing the outcome of a health issue, the loss of a loved one, or whatever set of circumstances that might lead to confrontation.

Ask yourself if there is anything you are presently being confronted by? What does it look like? What does it feel like?

Is there a need to depend on someone by your side to give you courage during this time? If your strength comes from someone or something, place that idea on the back burner for the next few moments.

As you stand alone with this confrontation, it may seem like you are alone, but you are not. Inner strength is there for you, and is a lot stronger than you think. Any feelings of weakness you may have may be coming from your outer self expressing the fear and doubt.

Close your eyes and separate your outer self from your inner Self. Let your mind be empty, and let yourself just BE. If that's hard to do, then imagine you are riding on a twig that is being carried quickly downstream in a rushing brook. (The twig is your outer self.) The strength of the moving water passes by everything along the way. You are not afraid of any obstacles as you ride on the twig. Feel the strength of the water. (The moving water is your inner Self.)

Right here and right now claim that strength. Don't depend solely on the twig to get you where you need to go. The twig could eventually float off course and wind up drifting aimlessly in a shallow pool. The twig was able to travel as far as it did because it was riding on the inherent inner strength of the moving water. The twig managed to meet all obstacles along the way.

It takes practice to mentally hold on to that inner strength when needed, but it's worth it. My suggestion is to perpetually picture the brook as power. Don't let the brook dry up and become lifeless. Your thoughts can make all the difference. You may even go a few thoughts further and let the brook flow into a vast body of water that manifests all the strength there is. It never runs out.

You may say that this thought is not practical and what does it have to do with courage? The answer is "nothing". It's just an exercise to get you to look beyond your outer self and see a part of you that is stronger than you think. It's a matter of changing your thoughts regardless of outcomes.

I can think of many times I have been confronted during my life. I'm sure you can as well. Where did you get the needed strength?

When you select the *Courage* card, think of ways you can draw on that inner strength. Think of all the areas you demonstrate that strength, and practice applying inner strength to various challenges you might face.

Questions

1. What is holding you back from having the courage you need?

2. Do you believe in yourself?

3. Are you willing to take the risk involved in searching for what you might find within yourself?

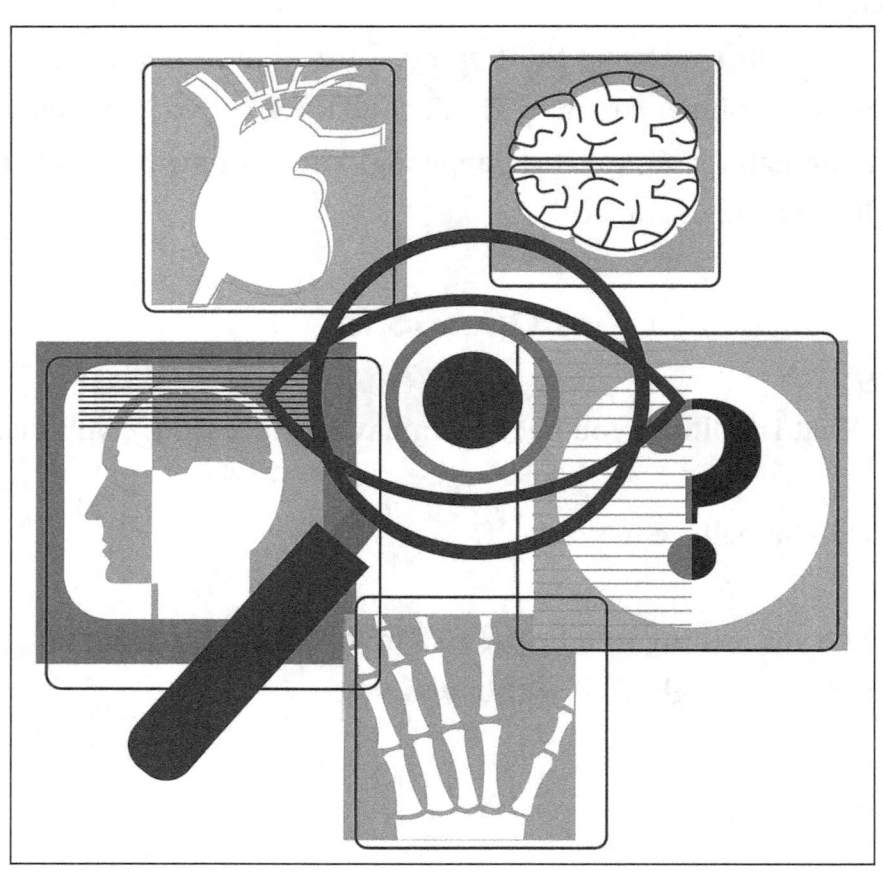

Understanding

Understanding put into practice is what makes changes. Today's challenges with understanding can lead to stability.

With regard to health, I am frequently asked, "Why? Why is it that I feel the way I do? Why does this happen to me? What caused this to happen?" Sometimes the answers come easy and sometimes they don't. Each person is basically the same and yet different. We all have a heart, lungs, gut, kidneys, etc. What makes it different is what triggers our physiology to respond differently than the next person. Understanding these "whys" has led me to a greater understanding of the functions of the human body and the role a mental outlook plays in physiology.

Teaching someone to understand themselves or to understand others takes a lot of observation and detective work. However, by daily observing your personal responses and outcomes, you can become your own best detective.

Most people just take for granted that someone else should fix them. Of course, it also depends on the nature of what needs to be fixed. Others truly want to know "why" in order to apply self-help. Start by searching for those answers not found in books. Answers often come from that deep inner voice of your mind that speaks to you in the stillness -or- from the constant chatter that cannot let the mind quiet down. Both situations are important for self-understanding.

Body language and functions may describe what could be going on in the mind. Some examples are: anxiety, tightness in the abdomen, diarrhea that comes up with fear, stress or even craving chocolate. The list goes on and on.

You may ask, "How about a recurrent physical symptom that doesn't seem to have any real situation connected to it?" A quick common response often encountered is, "I didn't do anything. It just happened." OK. Either accept that reason as…just that –or- work on an understanding of what may have preceded the situation or circumstance immediately prior or even several days before. Any recurrent set of symptoms can have more than one component. Yes, it could just be physical, but often anything that returns repeatedly usually has a mental component. The mind/body connection is real.

Today's challenges with understanding can lead to stability even when an ongoing physical condition has progressed and appears to be irreversible. With understanding, a personal effort might be the key to stopping the process or at least, slowing things down. I have seen others who have been so powerful in their minds that healings have occurred without any outward physiological intervention.

Personal observations and putting "two and two" together enlighten us to many benefits. Such benefits can be peace of mind, an acceptance of causes, and the willingness to change.

Understanding allows for better relationships because it changes one's self to view a new perspective, which can make all the difference.

When you read this *Pick-of-the-Day*! get yourself into a space of feeling. What is your whole physical body saying about how it feels? Does it feel relaxed? Does it feel tense? Does it feel congested? Is there a pressure feeling anywhere? Once you have done that, is there an emotion attached to that feeling? Is the emotion negative, such as, frustration, anger, fear, or sadness? Or is the emotion positive, like calmness, joy, love or excitement?

If you find yourself focusing on a specific body part, stop and wait. What are you thinking? Do not be judgmental. Just observe your thoughts. You don't have to be a rocket scientist to know whether your thoughts are good, bad or indifferent. Your inner conscience knows how to interpret them. Understanding put into practice is what makes changes. Reflect on your observations.

The human body is a wonderful vehicle. It takes us so many places and with its help, reveals to our minds the avenues necessary to heal ourselves on levels that facilitators cannot reach.

With this awareness, changes take place. My challenge to you is to have an understanding of who you are. If you don't like what you observe, only you have the power and the ability to change it. If you like what you see, you also have the power and ability to nurture it.

When you pick the *Understanding* card, add the components of feeling and emotion into the equation of your thoughts. Remind yourself each day to observe what is revealed. Journaling is a helpful tool to note progress.

Don't forget to give thanks for new and old insights. Watch yourself enfold.

Questions

1. What did you learn being an observer of yourself?

2. What are you going to do about it?

3. Are you going to hold on to the experience or the response, or use it as a guide for healing?

> ## Wisdom
>
> *Your experiences can help
> build a better life.
> Life is a learning and growing process.
> Today, find something
> new to learn about.*

Experts in every field have spent dedicated hours in the process of learning.

Gaining wisdom was one of the major priorities of Confucius, a great educator and scholar of his time. Confucius taught that inner Wisdom, individual integrity and education promoted great leaders in government, business, and family affairs.

However, many other great philosophers believed that Self-Wisdom gave one power, and that this type of Wisdom brought unity to all areas of life. Therefore, wisdom isn't necessarily just an intellectual process, but a knowingness that is built into our intellect. That makes Wisdom a part of us that knows that it knows. It's a part of us that dialogues with our inner voice. We all have had conversations with this inner voice, so you know exactly what I'm talking about. To explain it any further would put a limitation to the depths of knowingness.

It's the same Wisdom that is built into your personal genetic code and cell membranes, but more than that, it is a Wisdom that abides in what has been formulated within your unique Innate Intelligence.

Wisdom of the Self is an empowering asset and is allied with the power to overcome virtually any obstacle. This internal mechanism can differentiate what works and what doesn't work for you.

Wisdom of the Self is the most important card in the deck. It's the key to the whole deck of cards.

It's not enough to just get up each day, do your job, feed the dog, and take care of the family. More importantly, our inner Self needs a daily mental inventory to process our experiences, which helps build and nurture a better life. In other words, find out what makes you tick. We all have different motivational drives and goals, but to unfold life's experiences to become in harmony with the outer and inner Self is paramount. Taking responsibility for the self is the wisdom that empowers. Self-Wisdom is the built-in common denominator in each one of us.

I believe that intuition is linked in some way to Wisdom. How does that statement intuitively feel to you? Does it create a feeling of knowing what's right or is there self-doubt? If self-doubt comes into the picture you may be thinking from the ego mind (outer self) rather than your inborn Innate Intelligence (inner Self). Philosophers and theologians refer to this as "getting your nothingness out of the way to make room for the Divine".

Close your eyes for a moment. Ask the outer self (ego) to step aside. As you do this, allow your outer self to be an observer of this wonderful being that you really are. Allow your inner Self to guide you in the Wisdom the outer self needs, wants and desires. When you return to your outer self, bring the tools revealed in the recesses of your inner mind and go forth with that as your guidance.

When you select the *Wisdom* card remember there are two parts to you ... the outer and the inner. Each contains wisdom. One area of wisdom is acquired and the other area is inherited. Acquired wisdom deals with the accumulation of everything you have been exposed to since birth. Inherited Wisdom is that Innate Intelligence that knows that it knows. I know, beyond a shadow of a doubt, that you know the difference I'm talking about.

Questions

1. Do you have difficulty listening to this inner Wisdom? If you do, test it on small things first.

2. Have you ever had the experience that something inside told you not to do something and you did it anyway?

3. Did the outcome of that decision turn out to be for your highest and best good? Or, did you end up with regrets that needed to be rectified because you didn't listen to the inner Self?

> **Kindness**
>
> *Today, make it a point to be kind.*
> *Any intolerance reflects in your*
> *personal well-being.*

What is kindness anyway? Kindness can wear many hats. It can be politeness to others, the way we think or act towards others, how generous we are and feel, or even how we treat *ourselves*. Intolerance reflects in your personal well-being. It's like looking into a mirror. What you see is what you get!

Do you have a habit of looking at others and then find yourself being judgmental about something -or- is kindness a way of life? How do you re-act to family, co-workers, strangers and/or telemarketers? Do you *only* display kindness when you want something? That makes kindness conditional! Kindness, like love, must be unconditional!

Now, think about…what *does* kindness feel like on both the giving and receiving ends?

Others have told me, "I tried to be kind, but what did I get back? Nothing, but misery." "People have taken advantage of me." "I've been treated like a doormat, so why bother?" And, then others have said, "Sometimes it's a challenge to be kind, but it's worth it." Receiving kindness can also be difficult for some. Are you one those personalities? For some, it is easier to give than receive. Why?

Kindness is liken to the law of attraction. If you have a weak magnet, it'll only attract a little. If the magnet is stronger, it will attract more. One of the things that immediately came to my mind was the magnetic rails for high-speed trains. What are the odds of the train jumping the track when the force is so strong?

The body/mind connection is very real with the trait of kindness. Unconditional acts of kindness create a homeostatic consistency resulting in a state of equilibrium, which releases tension and stress. Otherwise, either kindness or unkindness based on conditional outcomes can play havoc with our body's physiology causing tension and stress.

Scientific researchers tell us that immune responses are affected by our nervous system. The nervous system also responds to our emotions and how we think about things. Are you tricking the body/mind connection by the way you think and feel? If so, then trick it into a healthful state of well-being. Be and do what you want to become! Be a magnetic force.

Kindness provides a feedback that feels good, and you will know it. You don't have to be told if you were kind or unkind because your own body/mind response knows that it knows.

My challenge to you is to be aware of kindness to yourself and others. Make it part of a lifestyle commitment. Soon the world will seem so much brighter. Any enthusiasm and motivation that has been missing will regenerate.

When you select the *Kindness* card, let it be a reminder to make kindness a way of life. You'll be wearing an inner smile that only you can know for sure!

Questions

1. Can you improve your kindness to others and to yourself? If not, why not?

2. What would you lose, if you were kind?

3. Are you willing to accept the outcomes of kind actions? Remember, be unconditional.

> **Keep it to Yourself**
>
> *Do a good thing for someone every day and don't let anyone know about it!*

How well do you keep secrets? I'm not referring to confidential information you may be entrusted with as part of your job. Let's separate ourselves for a moment between business and personal lives. The type of secret I'm referring to is something you do, or have done, for someone else. Who else really needs to know about something you have accomplished that helped someone or improved a situation?

Some examples of unnecessary good deeds might be carrying a package for someone that appears to be struggling, cleaning up an untidy area in a public place, giving a homeless person something to eat, or seeing an opportunity to be of service.

Think back, when was the last time you did something good for someone and just kept it to yourself? Sooner or later did you find yourself telling someone else about it? Examine that need. Was it for approval? Were you seeking credit? Did you want the person you told to think of you as a "nice guy"?

There are many advisors who tell us we need to "blow our own horns because, if we don't, no one else will." Give credit where credit is due. But, instead, this exercise may be a step towards finding greater humility.

There is a bumper sticker that says, "Practice Random Acts of Kindness". That actually says it quite well. I've known a few people with those stickers on their cars, but at the same time would boast about their acts of kindness. Questioning their motives, questioned my own views and feelings about the purpose of these random acts. Was I being judgmental of someone's acts of kindness? What was in it for them? That opened up a can of worms for me.

The final analysis was to just BE. It really doesn't matter after all what is said and done. What does matter is how you feel about helping someone else. My suggestion with this *Pick-of-the Day!* card is to help someone without receiving any recognition for it and see how that settles within your own being. Do what feels right to you, whether you end up sharing your experience or not.

When you select the *Keep it to Yourself* card, try holding on to that good feeling as long as you can. See how long you can keep a secret. Will it be an hour, a day, a week or more? Or will it just fade away into lost memories never to resurface again?

Questions

1. Do you already do things for others? Why do you do them?

2. If you don't do things to help others, what is your reasoning behind it?

3. The next time an opportunity comes up that Innately feels right, do it without a second thought and see what happens.

> ## Comfort
>
> *You have the ability within yourself to comfort someone by listening without judgment.*

Providing comfort without judgment can be a tall order. It takes much self-discipline to listen to others quietly with an open mind. Many times we formulate responses in our minds even before the other person stops talking. We all make assumptions of what the other person's world should look like based on our own values.

Judgments are pervasive in our society. It appears that the media focuses on who is to blame for everything. How do we get off this "merry-go-round"? Maybe it's time to remember the "buck stops here" and forget the "blame game".

Listening without judging not only comforts the other person, it can also bring you comfort from knowing that you have not added to the problem by focusing on any perceived wrongdoing.

Think for a moment of a time when someone else judged you. How did that feel? What emotions were stirred? Chances are the feelings and emotions lingered for a while. Sometimes judgments create a damaging sore spot that remains indefinitely.

Comforting someone doesn't necessarily mean condoning the person's action or behavior. By just listening, you allow the other person to vent his or her frustrations. Many times the comfort other people receive from your listening can calm them down enough to see their own situation more clearly.

What's in it for you, the provider of the comfort? It's a measure of personal growth. It's seeing the person you have comforted with eyes and ears that have matured in understanding.

Challenge yourself not to react or make snap judgments. It's a comfort to yourself to be able to rise above certain situations that would have previously "pushed buttons".

Internal comfort resonates peace. Peace resonates comfort. Are you ready to add more peace within yourself? It may be what's needed to change an attitude. Listen to your own body language. As you do this, can you feel the comfort within yourself? Often it is accompanied by a deep sighing breath, which is a sign of release.

When you have comforted someone by listening without judgment, give yourself a pat on the back because it took a lot of effort to accomplish that task. I call it a task because it takes effort and effort requires work. There are plenty of opportunities to practice your comforting skills.

When you select the *Comfort* card, find some way to remind yourself not to have an opinion of what others should or should not do. You don't have to agree or disagree. Just listen, and have a great day!

Questions

1. Are you overlooking opportunities to comfort without judgment?

2. Are you aware of how it feels when someone judges you? If so, transfer those feelings and image how others feel when they are on the receiving end of any judgments.

3. Ask yourself at the end of the day, how it felt to be a comfort to someone else and listen without judgment.

> **Trust**
>
> *It's a privilege to be trusted.*
> *With that privilege it reveals insights*
> *about yourself and others.*

In general, we trust a number of people who represent major businesses. We trust airlines or we would not fly. We trust banks or we would not deposit our hard-earned money and use checking accounts. (Remember, I said "in general") We trust manufacturers or we wouldn't buy their products. However, I have often heard people tell me, "I don't know who to trust or believe anymore", directing this statement towards specific individuals just outside their small circles. There is a fear when walking in dimly lit areas or travelling alone in some situations. In today's society many people are being taught not to trust anyone for fear of getting hurt. It's considered a personal safety issue.

The great Chinese philosopher, Confucius, taught his students that we ourselves must be what we expect others to be. If you expect honesty, you must also be honest. If you expect others to be accountable, you must also be accountable. Confucius emphasized being an example. He taught those qualities to leaders in government. Even though his teachings dated circa 520 B.C.E., his morals and ethics can still be applied today. He taught about unchanging natural law and its principles derived from right reason.

Therefore, when someone *does* trust you, you must be doing something right.

The trust you seek is seeking you. Learn to trust your instincts and when it feels right there's a sense of responsibility in following through with that natural Innate impulse.

How does it feel to be trusted by someone or even to trust yourself? Does this trust give you a sense of confidence? Or, does it hold up a red flag that says STOP, which turns you into a defensive mode? Or, does trust fill you with an assurance of strength? Remember, you create feelings and emotions by your thinking.

Self-evaluation is not always the easiest thing to do. It's a lot easier to first evaluate what revolves around you. Ask yourself if your immediate environment is running smoothly or is there a certain amount of chaos? Then, listen to your instincts or conscience regarding the ups and downs you may be experiencing. Your reactions to situations can reveal whether outside influences are what is directing you or whether you are trusting your Innate.

Being responsible to yourself is a good place to start. Be a magnet to attract the good. Practice what you want to become.

When the *Trust* card is selected, remember the privilege that goes along with being trustworthy. It's a privilege that is granted by virtue of natural law, which is binding in human society.

Questions

1. What percentage of the time do you experience trust in others? If there is no trust, why or why not?

2. Have you been conditioned not to trust anyone or anything?

3. Most of all, can you trust yourself? If you do, what makes you that way? If not, why not?

> **Decision Making**
>
> *Before making an important decision, release all resentment, despair and self-pity.*
> *Don't let your ego mind lead you astray.*

There will be numerous occasions in the course of our lives when important decisions must be made. Unfortunately, some of life's critical decisions must be made during times of crisis. However, many times when fear steps in, we allow circumstances to dictate our choices. It is best to make decisions when functioning with a clear mind. It's difficult at times not to be distracted by the ego part of your mind, which sometimes acts out of resentment, despair or self-pity. The key is to recognize when you are in that state of mind because decisions made for wrong reasons usually come back to haunt us.

Working on self-improvement every day can guide you to a Wisdom that is part of your Innate conscience birthright. Deep within there is a part that knows that it knows, and can recognize the answers by your physical body responses. You may feel relaxed and calm in one situation, yet tense and uncomfortable in another. Learn to identify body language. It will help guide you when making decisions. Ignoring the body's messages and signs may mislead the mind and create a battlefield between the body/mind connection.

Practicing this method in little things can help identify where reactions and decisions originate. The goal is to release any resentments, despair or self-pity in order for right decision making to take place. Doing this for little decisions will make it easier when you are faced with important big decisions. Like anything else, it takes practice until it becomes a habit.

Finally, how did it feel knowing you made a good decision? What emotion surfaced? Did you wrestle with your inner thoughts or did the decision come naturally without struggle?

We all possess inner qualities that resonate with peace, joy and harmony. We must find those attributes that speak to us. They will tell us what choices to make in order to avoid "paying the price" later.

When you select the *Decision Making* card…stop, look and listen where your inner voice is coming from.

Questions

1. Do you live your life in a constant state of crisis management?

2. What can you do to make life run more smoothly so that when an important decision needs to be made, it can be done more easily?

3. Are you willing and able to evaluate your life without the ego getting in the way?

> **Priorities**
>
> *Today, focus on the priority of the day,
> taking a break, as needed,
> to revitalize yourself.*

The clock is ticking and you're running around like a chicken with its head cut off. The "things-to-do list" is so long that you are undecided what to do first. There are deadlines to meet, but your actions are scattered in many different directions.

Or maybe that's not your challenge. Maybe it's working on health issues and you are being treated for a whole list of symptoms that won't resolve.

Or, maybe there's an exciting event about to take place, for example, a wedding or moving into a new home.

Overwhelming priorities come in all shapes and sizes.

No matter what the priority is or how you look at it…the body doesn't differentiate the stressor. It doesn't make any difference to the body's nervous system and hormonal secretions because it tends to react in the same way. (If you are really interested in knowing more details about the body's stress response, I refer you to Robert Sapolsky's 1998 book *Why Zebras Don't Get Ulcers, An Updated Guide to Stress, Stress-Related Diseases, and Coping*.)

I'm not saying throw up your hands in despair if you have a hard time coping with priorities. Take the time to look at each priority from a different perspective. This will help you feel more in control of your reactions in a situation rather than the situation controlling you.

I once had a doctor tell me, "What difference is it going to make a hundred years from now." We will always have deadlines to meet and challenges to face, but what I learned from this doctor's comment was I had to work on myself daily in order to not react in ways that put myself into crisis situations that could have been prevented. With forethought in handling challenges, learning to say "yes" or "no" when evaluating the priorities, I was able to temporarily place them on the back burner while empowering myself in the process.

Depending on the circumstances, taking a break, whether it be for a few moments during the day, or taking a vacation break, or even a sabbatical, can revitalize one's self.

If the need is a daily break, sit or rest for 15 or 20 minutes. You will be surprised at the benefit it brings. Some people try to cram too much into their lunch hour that it defeats the purpose of having a break. Quieting the mind and the body allows your physiology to re-energize and be "powered-up" for what's at hand. Of course, if too many "time-outs" are taken, it can also be a sign of procrastination. I am assuming you are basically a healthy person. Watch out for developing patterns during times of priorities.

On the other side of the coin, there are others who thrive on stressors. I know lots of people like that. Eventually, according to some researchers, unrelenting stress is what brings on "burn out". There isn't any more energy stored to be able to accomplish anything. Chronic fatigue is what the picture may look like.

If the issues are work and/or career related, there are many self-help books on time management you can turn to.

If the issues are health challenges, ask yourself if a lifestyle change is needed? Are you getting enough sleep? Do you need to get 8 hours of sleep every night? Does your diet need to improve? How about regular exercise? If you are not sure what needs to be addressed, seek out professional help.

Whatever is causing excess stress as a result of overextending priorities, seek new ways to manage your life and activities.

Another approach to managing priorities is to see them as completed and resolved in your mind's eye. For some unknown reason, doing this seems to help recognize what needs to be done. Opportunities seem to show up with clarity. Your mind/body connection will thank you for these various approaches.

When you pick the *Priorities* card, keep the desired end results in your thoughts. Staying focused brings you closer to your accomplishments. Refresh your mind with short periods of rest to re-energize. Smile and pat yourself on the back for a job well done.

Questions

1. Do you feel like you are always juggling priorities?

2. Take the time to make a list of everything that's on your mind. Next, divide the list into what aspect of your life it pertains to, for example: work, education, family, health, leisure time, etc. Are your activities demonstrating a balanced lifestyle?

3. With each list that you make, look at what needs to be completed and resolved in the order of importance. Were you able to re-evaluate your priorities more easily?

> **Undesired Project**
>
> *Get through it in smaller increments.*
> *Set a timer for 30 minutes and*
> *stay focused on the project.*
> *Repeat until done in a suitable schedule.*

The first thing that comes to mind is "What is exactly an undesired project?" It could be a chore; a type of job that needs to be done that doesn't have fun attached to it; something that needs to be organized. It can be anything that brings on procrastination.

For most people, when the project is completed, it is accompanied with a sense of satisfaction. Whether it is a short or long assignment, a place to start is not with the amount of work or effort required, but seeing the completion in your mind's eye. Holding on to that vision generates motivation.

What if your "things to do" project list is so long that you just don't know where to begin? What works for me is to create lists into short-term and long-term goals. These ideas are comparable to others who teach organizational skills. However, my biggest friend that helps me get through it all is a kitchen timer. I have several timers throughout my home and office. My projects, whether they are desirable or undesirable, would never get done unless I get started. A motivation to begin is to allot 30 minutes to the job I want to accomplish…then I stop. I continue in 30 minute increments until the project is completed. I prefer not to work on the assignment again until either the next day or when I have the time to devote another 30 minute segment. Sometimes the projects may take days, weeks or even months. This method improves my work because I become focused. It changes my outlook toward the work and my attitude automatically changes.

Address any project with a plan by turning it into a game. Most people like games because they can uplift their feelings and spirit. With an uplifted attitude, these 30-minute increments will go by quickly and with it will come the satisfaction of accomplishment.

Sometimes a project needs to be done by someone else because you lack a needed skill. Take that same focused time to look for suitable people to hire.

It's also fun to take a magic marker and cross out accomplished tasks in the "things to do" list. Even though it's psychological, the more items I mark off my list, the more I know I am achieving my goals. Periodically, I'll make a new list and carry over anything not completed.

This method has worked for others as well. It has helped me "not to beat myself up" if things are still pending because I know I'm working on the project until completion.

The other valuable thing I have learned from this exercise is the need for balanced living. Admitting to be a workaholic my whole life, prioritizing time allotments has helped me create that balance. What are your priorities? The main thing is to identify them.

When the *Undesired Project* card is selected, see the end result and start in small increments of time until completion. Observe how good it feels to do something about it. It's a recipe for successful completion of your project. Life is like a game and it's all about how you play it! Practice methods that enhance work improvement. Create an attitude with a positive outlook. Admire your finished project. You deserve it. It's a job well done!

Questions

1. Ask yourself if you are a chronic procrastinator, or have too many projects and don't know where to begin?

2. Are you willing to stop complaining about stuff that needs to be done? Of course, that's if you have a propensity to be that type of person. Ask yourself, are you that type of person?

3. Are you dependent on others to do the work for you? If so, find ways to manage or delegate.

Laughing

*Find something to laugh about.
It will wake up
the sleeping parts within you.*

Has anyone ever said to you, "I haven't heard you laugh that hard in a long time." Pay attention to the next time you have a good laugh. I bet it released a lot of stress. Sometimes I've had patients tell me they are not sure what worked best, the treatment they were given or the good laugh they had when they came into the office. All of us like to be around a light atmosphere. Norman Cousins once did some research on laughter with patients who were given a life-threatening diagnosis. Laugh therapy changed the lives of many people resulting in better mental and physical states of well-being. Laughter is part of any healing process.

My husband and I have a mini-schnauzer. There is always something to laugh about each day. "Joey da Fonz" lightens up our lives every day, in fact many times a day. For those of you who have a dog, I'm sure you have many stories that have made you laugh.

Pause for a moment to recall a time when you have had a good laugh. Recreate that moment. Your own thinking about the reason for the laughter is what "tickled your funny bone".

Make laughter an everyday event by finding something to laugh about. Wake up the sleeping parts within you. When body-parts become dysfunctional for long periods of time, they start to break down. Staying active is one of the keys to wellness. That's one reason why exercise has become so popular.

We have diets to better our health, exercise to keep us in shape, sleep to regenerate ourselves. There is also leisure time and vacation for balance. Why not make laughter part of a routine if you find you are not laughing enough?

Some people take life too seriously and do not give themselves permission to be humorous. If you are experiencing difficulty or pain in your life, it's still OK to laugh. Laughing inappropriately at times, however, must be answered within by your own conscience. You will know when things are not so funny.

When you finish reading this topic, look for something to laugh about. Don't put it off. Find humor in something right now. Putting things off may be a sign of procrastination. Finding a way to be present in each moment, including the funny parts, can help you to focus on the here and now.

When the *Laughing* card is selected, immediately smile and be ready for opportunities to see humor around you. Lighten up!

Questions

1. Do you find yourself saying, "I don't have time for that." Are you considered "too serious"?

2. How does it feel to be around people who are cheerful and enjoy life? How does it feel to be around people who drain your energy?

3. Are you someone who already laughs a lot? If not, get a dog!

Contentment

*Contentment comes from an inner satisfaction.
It does not depend on what others think or say.*

Being true to oneself can bring contentment, but it isn't always easy when we live in a world of "shoulds" and "should nots".

Why are we confronted with so many rules and regulations? Is it because we have lost our way and everything is for the ego's protection? What is it that we keep defending? What is it that we keep justifying? What is satisfaction anyway?

The human psyche seems to be continually searching for approval from the outside in order to feel satisfied. It wants to achieve, accomplish and obtain material possessions.

In contrasting, the contentment that comes from inner satisfaction is not the same as achieving an accomplishment or obtaining physical things or possessions. It is a contentment that goes back to the roots of where we came from and generates inner peace.

Scientists are now telling us that we are made from the same particles that make up stars. It is with these physical components that bring us to an understanding that we are part of the big picture. But, even deeper than this material connection is a common

Intelligence that exists beyond any physical structure. This Intelligence is also part of who we are.

In many disciplines of study, this Intelligence is referred to as "consciousness". It also correlates with what physics refer to as "absolute space". This common quality is a feeling of pure, contented emptiness that runs through our minds when we are free of thoughts and allow ourselves to just BE. Identifying with this part of us brings about a contentment that cannot cause stress or judgment. It's like taking a wonderful vacation from the hustle and bustle of everyday life. This contentment takes us out of the trials and tribulations in the challenges that we meet daily.

How do you get to that place of inner satisfaction – that place of contentment? Some people find it easy to get there and others often struggle. Most of us enjoy flowers, so I am going to ask you to find a flower and just stare at it. As you focus only on the flower, examine all parts of it. Unite with the flower and pretend the flower has feelings and is content with just being a flower. Carry that feeling into yourself by being in that same space. Do nothing. Just BE.

Did you feel content to just linger there for a few seconds or a few minutes? Or, did you having difficulty quieting yourself? If so, that could be a sign of not experiencing that inner satisfaction. It may be a sign that you are going outside yourself to seek the contentment that is in the deeper part of you. This deeper part of you is the glue that holds you together, which is the same glue that holds the stars and the galaxies together. It's the invisible glue that trickles its way into everything that has ever been created.

Once you have identified and experienced this inner contentment, your life will never be the same. This awareness innately generates a satisfaction that helps you understand the true you. It also helps to understand others more clearly. It's like joining in cheer with the songs of the birds, or being one of the bubbles in a babbling brook, or part of the beauty, the fragrance and color of the flower you selected. It's knowing you are part of the whole cohesive system of everything there is.

As for me, I love the rose because it reminds me of all the facets of life including the thorns, which I see as representing life's challenges. When we hold the rose, we hold it carefully so as not to get pricked. Life is the same way. Handle it with care to enjoy the beauty and the sweetness.

The *Contentment* card requires that you think not only of the contentment derived from accomplishment, but also contentment that comes from knowing you are part of all there is. Allow your thinking to empty and just BE. Remember that just BEING, is the glue that connects everything together. Enjoy that place of contentment. It's a powerful space! It belongs to you!

Questions

1. Do you make a habit of not being content with yourself or with others?

2. Can you find contentment within yourself or are you dependent on what others think or say about you?

3. How often do you empty your mind of thoughts to go into that space of just BEING?

Stillness

Stilling the mind to experience the silence daily brings forth a Wisdom not found in books.

There are numerous "how to" books that teach variations on the subject of stilling the mind. You could say that this book falls into a similar category. Learning to practice this stillness, you will discover an enfolding Wisdom. A Wisdom that comes from a deeper connection found in the silence of *your own* mind. Revealing answers to burning questions about various aspects within the great school of life can be found by quietly listening to that inner voice.

This topic is most likely the toughest *Pick-of-the-Day!* especially if you are not used to stilling the mind. It takes a lot of practice to master, but may be the best investment of time you will ever make. The benefits derived are cumulative and liken to investing money at a bank that never stops earning interest well above "prime".

Here is one method that has worked for me and others I have taught.

Sit comfortably and command your body parts to relax. For example, say, "Feet relax." (Wait until they relax and then give the next command.) "Legs relax." (Wait again). Continue the process throughout the remainder of your body. Get the idea? Do this until you have an overall feeling of relaxation.

After you become both physically and mentally relaxed, bring a single object into your mind and concentrate on this object. Examples may be a flower, a gem, or a candle flame. It doesn't really matter what the object is because it's only to help you focus. Don't complicate the concentration. Just concentrate on one item.

Once you have settled in on the item, take it away in your mind. Now focus on your breath. As you breathe in and out slowly, take away the focus of your breath and become centered on the emptiness and stillness. Remain in that silence even if it's only for a few moments. Daily practice will eventually lengthen the time you spend there. Do not rush the process. You have now arrived at a place to seek the Wisdom not found in books. Now, from that place, ask yourself a question that needs an answer. Don't get hasty and put an answer in your mind. Just wait for an answer to filter in. If nothing happens, that's OK too. The answer might present itself at another time. It may come as an intuitive flash when you least expect it. When ready, slowly return your mind and body back to your immediate surroundings.

The whole process doesn't have to last more than 5-10 minutes. Making a habit to practice relaxation, concentration and emptying the mind can bring forth the benefits that only you are able to measure.

You don't have to be religious or spiritual to experience the stillness. All you have to be is willing to discover for yourself the Wisdom within your own consciousness. You can think of this quiet time as food for the inner Self, just like we need food for our bodies.

Some people call this meditation or contemplation. It doesn't have to have a fancy name. Call it anything you want. By practicing this daily, you will be able to quickly still your mind at will. It can enhance decision-making processes, solve problems from received insights, increase energy, balance physiology for improved health by releasing tension, and even improve relationships. The list is endless, but you'll never know the benefits of practicing stillness unless done regularly.

When the *Stillness* card is selected, let it be a reminder that it only takes about 5-10 minutes out of the day. The time spent is a valuable investment.

Questions

1. Ask yourself if there is a facet in your life that needs more focus to improve?

2. Are you ready to make the commitment to *Stillness* in order to stop the inner chatter and experience the silence?

3. If your answer to question 2 is…that you are too busy to take the time…then ask yourself if you are too busy to eat food every day for physical nourishment. Think of the stillness of silence as food for the mind.

> **Peace**
>
> *Being at peace within yourself contributes to world peace.*

The dictionary defines peace with many interpretations: 1) freedom from war, 2) harmony among people, 3) public order, 4) freedom from anxiety, annoyance or mental disturbance, 5) state of tranquility, 6) silence, 7) to make peace with one's self, and 8) a way of saying farewell.

I find the dictionary's order of definitions enlightening in itself. It starts outs out with the macrocosm down through and into the microcosm. How can the first definition happen without reversing the order? Peace within one's self through silence leads to tranquility. In turn, tranquility releases a mental disturbance of anxiety and annoyance, which can bring about harmony within your own life and those around you. Then, this inner peace can be brought into the world to live a peaceful co-existence.

The word…"world"… can mean the entire planet or it can be the world within the nucleus of the family, or the workplace or whatever revolves around your own environment.

Pick any definition of peace and see how you fit into that description. Does that definition resonate with your inner being?

What feelings come up for you when you pick one of the definitions?

It's difficult to have a finished product without the right ingredients. Maybe we will never see the first definition in our lifetime completely, but the place to start is within ourselves. We see glimpses of harmony through mass consciousness when people pull together all their efforts in times of natural disasters. When it comes to war, however, there appears to be much anger. Our inner strength needs to be cultivated by seeking that peace within ourselves.

The last definition in the dictionary is described as a way of saying farewell. That's a strong statement. How will you ultimately leave at that final moment? Will all the peace you have accomplished be satisfying enough? Is there anything you need to be at peace with?

The dictionary's first word is "freedom". What's holding you back from experiencing the freedom of inner peace?

When you select the *Peace* card, pick any definition and direct your thoughts and actions to establishing peace and freedom within. Adopting a peaceful lifestyle has many benefits. Also, as the body becomes more relaxed, it will function more efficiently.

Questions

1. What can you do right now to bring about more peace in your life?

2. Are you willing to take the steps in any resolution process to bring about that peace?

3. Can you achieve inner peace by yourself or do you need a mentor?

Intuition

*Listen to your inner voice
That is on the other side of your ego
(author unknown)*

Your inner voice is your own conscience speaking to you. It's not something that has developed as a result of the outer self. We all have had conversations with that part of our being. It's a part of us that knows that it knows. It's a part of us that if we listen carefully to it, can direct us in all facets of our lives.

Intuition can help us distinguish the difference between right and wrong, because it allows us to feel whether something is right or wrong.

We often hear of the expression, *"Let your conscience be your guide."* Conscience can move us in many directions. It can lead us to know our physical selves by paying attention to what and how we select foods in our diet, and/or the quantity of food necessary without over indulging. It can help us to exercise and know when we have had enough, if we listen. Otherwise, we could sustain an injury. This inner voice can tell us when it's time to rest and relax and to manage our lives effectively.

Listening to that inner voice can also apply to situations or persons outside ourselves. It can forewarn us of danger when it knocks at our door. Many people ignore that intuitive knock until after the fact, and then they comment that they should have paid more attention to their inner voice.

A mentor and teacher, Rev. Sharron Stroud called it the "Universe knocking". Each time the Universe knocks, it may get louder. If it knocks too loud and you don't pay attention to it, I can guarantee you; it will in some way get your attention!

Intuition is probably the most valuable inner tool that we possess. There's never a shortage, because *each person has their own intuition*.

When an intuitive thought comes to you, it's characterized as a "light bulb" going on in cartoons and a facial expression which perks up to listen. At that time, sharpen your senses to determine what that inner voice is really saying. Find ways within yourself to know what it feels like when this inner voice is speaking to you. Are you having a debate between your ego self and inner voice? Actually, is there a debate going on right now? Or have you developed the keen sense that the ego and inner self are in harmony?

Some people may say, "You must be crazy if you are talking to yourself". Just smile and know that these conversations with the inner Self empowers us to make right decisions when we can identify them as right feeling, right action and right purpose.

When you select the *Intuition* card, remember to be aware of the "Universe knocking". This inner voice is not the guest in your mind, it is the real you. The ego self is the guest.

Questions

1. Have you been denying access to this inner voice because of what others think or say you should be doing or experiencing?

2. Does this inner voice make you feel uncomfortable? If so, why?

3. Is it too difficult to pay attention to this inner voice? Is it because you haven't been able to trust your Innate? If so, then I suggest you re-read *Part I* of this book.

Appendix A

Sample of completed chart to tally your selections
CHART EXAMPLE FROM A CASE HISTORY

	TOPIC	1	2	3	4	5	6	7	8	9	10	11	12	13	14	15	16	17	18	19	20	21	22	23	24	25	26	27	28	29	30	31
2	Life is a game	■			■																											
4	Courage			■																	■					■						■
3	Peace					■										■									■							
7	Open Your Eyes						■	■					■									■	■				■			■		
3	Food for Thought										■	■		■																		
6	Trust														■		■	■						■				■			■	
2	Stillness																		■										■			
2	Kindness																			■									■			
1	Criticism																															

The 1st column shows the amount of times the card was selected during the course of a month. List the top 4:

Open Your Eyes (selected 7 times)
Trust (selected 6 times)
Courage (selected 4 times)
Peace and Food-for-Thought selected 3 times each. It was a tie)

Then look at the overall picture. See what it tells you.
Let Innate guide you on your inner work!

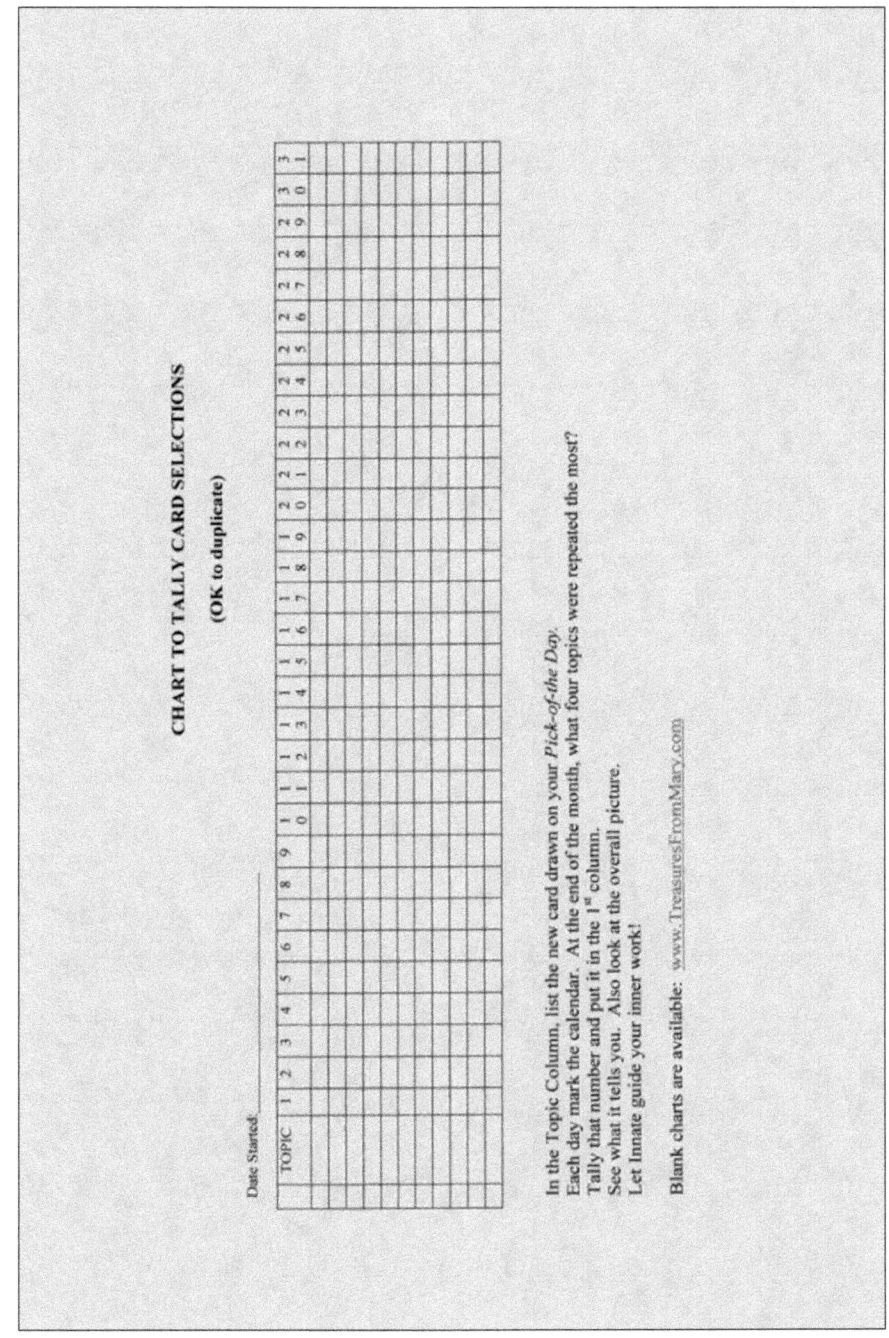

PART III

SELF-TALK

How to Use Part III

This section of the book will require a private personal investment of time. It is for the more serious minded person who wants to find a relationship with their physical symptoms and any specific accompanying mental/emotional components.

Examples of recurrent conditions might be: headaches, digestive disturbances, neck or back pain, colds and flu, fatigue, depression or any other physical symptoms you are experiencing, and what mental and/or emotional stressors are experienced simultaneously.

These exercises focus on your personal well-being with a body/mind/spirit connection allowing Innate to guide you. Get your ego out of the way.

By keeping a journal of correlated thoughts and experiences, and what you did each day to work on the physical conditions you selected, it will help patterns unfold and come into your awareness.

It is recommended that *Part III* be repeated more than once. It's a tool to be used throughout your lifetime.

What are you saying to yourself ?

Let us explore the following:

WE CANNOT GET AWAY FROM OURSELVES NO MATTER WHERE WE GO.

WHAT WE THINK AND SAY DETERMINES LIFE'S EXPERIENCES.

HOW TO IDENTIFY FEELINGS BOTH IN AND OUT OF YOUR COMFORT ZONE.

HOW TO TALK TO YOURSELF.

WE CANNOT GET AWAY FROM OURSELVES NO MATTER WHERE WE GO

From time to time have you ever said to yourself, "I've got to make some changes in my life", but for one reason or another, no change is made. Or, if you did do something different you found yourself back in the same old situations.

Maybe it has to do with lack of money, or maybe you can't make friends, or whatever the situation that you wanted changed or are running away from, seems to come back to haunt you over and over again.

One of the most common threads or refrains I've heard patients say is, "I thought when I divorced my spouse, my life was going to be totally different. And here I am, I attracted the same kind of person in my life."

Other examples could be related to health, family, career, personal motivation or just about any situation that needs a change. Why is it that some people cannot seem to be able to run away from the things that they want changed? Could it be that the change needs to first happen within before it can happen without? Set goals for positive change within yourself.

Or – you may have the response; "My life is running smoothly or perfectly". Forgive me, if I chuckle just a little. I don't know of anyone who doesn't have some inner work to do. It is my belief that we all have deep-seated questions that need answers and Innately, we can find those answers. Accessing this part of you entails trusting.

For this exercise be prepared with a notebook and pencil before starting. The best plan is to set aside about 90 minutes of uninterrupted time.

GET REAL COMFORTABLE IN YOUR FAVORITE CHAIR.

SLOWLY BREATHE IN AND OUT UNTIL YOU FEEL CALM.

DOING THIS EXERCISE IS NO ACCIDENTAL APPOINTMENT.

IT WILL TELL YOU "WHAT YOU ARE SAYING TO YOUR SELF."

THERE IS JUST YOU RIGHT NOW, SO….PUT EGO ASIDE, AND BE TOTALLY HONEST.

ARE YOU READY TO BE OPEN AND RECEPTIVE TO WHATEVER YOUR THOUGHTS, YOUR MIND, YOUR FEELINGS AND EMOTIONS ARE SAYING?

BEING ALONE FOR THIS EXERCISE IS A SAFE PLACE.

LET'S BEGIN.

PART III – SELF-TALK

In your notebook write down the first thoughts that come into mind when reading the following questions:

WHAT THOUGHTS ROUTINELY OCCUPY YOUR THINKING?
For example, does it involve health, money, relationships, peace of mind, self-esteem?
Whatever thought comes first in your mind, write it down.

HOW DID YOU EMOTIONALLY FEEL WHILE WRITING YOUR THOUGHTS?
Were you relaxed, happy, confident, tense, anxious, apprehensive, fearful, irritated, frustrated?
Whatever those feelings were, write them down.

DID YOU NOTICE ANY PARTICULAR PART OF YOUR BODY RESPOND TO THOSE FEELINGS OR EMOTIONS?
Close your eyes and concentrate. Do you, right now, feel one part of your body more than another? Is it your abdomen, heart, breathing, jaw, hands, feet, arms, legs? Is your body quiet and still, or does it feel nervous, achy, weak, bloated, puffy?
Just write down what you feel.

DO YOU OFTEN HAVE THOSE FEELINGS?
Answer: Yes, No or Sometimes? Whatever is appropriate.

Now take some deep breaths and release your mind from the questions just asked.

Make sure you clear your mind before continuing.

This next section describes an important concept. Even though the words are simple, it carries with it food for thought that must be grasped.

WHAT WE THINK AND SAY DETERMINES LIFE'S EXPERIENCES

To create anything, it starts with a thought or idea, which eventually manifests into form. **Here are some examples:**

Example: You want to grow tomatoes. You begin with an idea of planting tomatoes. You go to the store and buy a package of seeds, prepare the soil, and plant the seeds. The planted seeds know exactly what to do. Part of the process is watering the plants and giving it nutrients. By a natural law it produces tomatoes. It didn't mature into anything else. It didn't yield oranges, grapefruits or anything else. Just tomatoes.

Let's take another example.

Example: You want to make ice cubes to put into a drink. Let's look at the process involved. First came the thought or idea that you wanted to make ice cubes. You go to the sink and fill the ice cube tray with water, then put the water into the freezer. The laws of physics go to work because of the mechanism built into the freezer. What's next? You eventually get ice cubes. It didn't create anything else! It only created ice cubes. The process was taken for granted.

This time let's take another example using man's thought:

Example: Think back when you had a great accomplishment happen in your life and the attitude you had. Your goal was envisioned before the end result materialized. **Man's thought follows a mental law and produces whatever you think or say.** We cannot continually say one thing and expect something else to manifest. The end result will always be whatever seed you planted in your soil of thinking.

What do these three examples have in common?

1. Everything ever created starts with a thought.
2. The thought is set into motion, whether by the force of a natural law, a physical law or a mental law.
3. The action of the law builds up a momentum and manifests the end result. It's known as cause and effect.

There is yet another process. That process involves <u>listening</u> to the Universal Intelligence that reciprocates by filling our Innate Intelligence with the characteristic qualities of personality to become the person which changes the blueprint that our ego mind has allowed ourselves to become. It's a transcendence that goes beyond cause and effect, and comes from a place of the creative cosmos to express itself.

If this process is not grasped, don't worry. It will come to you in time especially if you commit to entering the silence of your mind. Why? Because by emptying your mind and listening, you will transcend in consciousness, which is yet another law. Let's call it spiritual law. (Do not confuse or equate spiritual law with the laws of organized religions.) The main point here is to first embody the concept that everything starts with a thought, and by repeatedly having the same thought, the process begins to manifest automatically. This means you have cultivated the thought. Without focus, the thought dies on the vine. The natural, physical and mental laws all work as a result of cause and effect. Spiritual law pre-exists the results of cause and effect.

After understanding the sequence of the three common points, as aforementioned, let's now move into the next section.

> "Man, by thinking, can bring into his experience whatsoever he desires…and becomes a living embodiment of his thoughts."
>
> Ernest Holmes

PART III – SELF-TALK

Let's go to a life experience as an example.
Write down something you accomplished and really felt good about.

DID YOU HAVE A VISION OF THIS ACCOMPLISHMENT BEFORE IT ACTUALLY HAPPENED? *Write down your vision.*

DID YOU HAVE A SPECIFIC FEELING ABOUT THE ACCOMPLISHMENT BEFORE IT HAPPENED?
Write down your feelings.

COULD YOU SEE YOURSELF ACCOMPLISHING THIS TASK?
Yes or No?

WHAT WERE YOU DOING WHEN YOU COULD SEE YOURSELF WORKING ON THE TASK? *Write it down.*

DID YOU HAVE ALL THE STEPS WRITTEN DOWN AHEAD OF TIME BEFORE THE TASK WAS ACCOMPLISHED?
Yes or No?

DID YOU JUST START YOUR TASK WITHOUT BEING SURE WHAT THE STEPS WERE?   Yes or No?

HOW DID YOU PROCEED?   *Write it down.*

WHAT WAS YOUR DRIVING FORCE?   *Write it down.*

> "Thank God every morning when you get up that you have something to do which must be done, whether you like it or not. Being forced to work, and forced to do your best, will breed in you temperance and self control, diligence of will, cheerfulness and content, and a hundred virtues which the idle will never know."
>
> Charles Kingsley
>
> *Doing something is taking action.*
> *If you never take the initiative, you will never experience what you want.*
> *No thought....no action....creates inaction.*

PART III – SELF-TALK

> "All causes are essentially mental, and whosoever comes into daily contact with a high order of thinking must take on some of it."
>
> Charles Fillmore
>
> *Since all causes are mental, if you think daily thoughts of a higher consciousness, you will take on those aspects in your life.*

> "Have a bias toward action....let's see something happen now. You can break that big plan into small steps and take the first step right away."
>
> Richard Thalheimer
>
> *Act....Start....even if you don't have the steps laid out. The original plan will create the end result if you keep your goal and mind focused.*

> "Every suggested idea produces a corresponding physical reaction....Every idea constantly repeated ends by being engraved upon the brain, provoking the act which corresponds to the idea."
>
> Scott Reed
>
> *Every idea produces a corresponding physical reaction. Our brain is a storehouse just like a computer. It will keep spitting out what is stored. There's an old computer saying, "Garbage in, garbage out." Program your computer with what you want in your print out of life.*

HOW TO IDENTIFY FEELINGS
BOTH IN AND OUT OF YOUR COMFORT ZONE

Body language gives us information about ourselves. Alice Steadman, in her book, *Who's the Matter with Me? (1969)*, states: "The inner man is in constant conversation with the outer man. The body becomes a battleground of arguments and a site of peace treaties."

In my career as a chiropractic doctor I have taken thousands of patient case histories to ultimately pinpoint the etiologies of where aches and pains originate. Unless there has been a specific incident like a fall, an auto accident or some other trauma, I'm amazed at the most common answer.

What do you think is the answer?

STRESS

Common statements heard from patients are:

"WHEN I'M UNDER STRESS, MY STOMACH ACHES"
"WHEN I'M UNDER STRESS, I CAN'T BREATHE."
"WHEN I'M UNDER STRESS, MY NECK HURTS."
"WHEN I'M UNDER STRESS, I GET TENSION HEADACHES."
"WHEN I'M UNDER STRESS, I GET CHEST PAINS."

The list goes on and on . . .

PART III – SELF-TALK

Complete the following statements in your notebook. List at least three examples.

When I'm under stress _____.
When I'm under stress _____.
When I'm under stress _____.

Common responses to emotional hurts have been:

"WHEN I GET UPSET, I CAN'T EAT OR I GET DIARRHEA."
"WHEN I GET UPSET, I GET ANGRY AND THEN I GET NERVOUS AND/OR IRRITATED."
"WHEN I GET UPSET I CRY. THEN AFTERWARDS I USUALLY FEEL RUN DOWN AND GET A COLD."

Again this list goes on and on . . .

Complete the following statements. List at least three examples.

When I get upset _____.
When I get upset _____.
When I get upset _____.

Other examples of common comments:

"SHE MAKES ME SICK."
"HE'S A PAIN IN MY NECK."
"MY BOSS EXPECTS TOO MUCH OUT OF ME."
"MY NERVES ARE GETTING THE BEST OF ME."
　　　　　　　　The lists are endless . . .

The brain is like a recorder and the more you make statements like those mentioned above, the more it becomes embedded into memory cells. Our cells, including glands, have recorded all of our past thoughts, emotions and experiences. Repeated irritations cause dysfunction, which can eventually turn into pathology. When the mind and body have a conflict, you become symptomatic expressive.

Readers who would like more details on the physiology of what happens under stress, I refer you to *Why Zebras Don't Get Ulcers, an Updated Guide to Stress, Stress-Related Diseases and Coping* (1998) by Robert M. Sapolsky, Professor of Biological Sciences and Neuroscience at Stanford University.

If you can catch the feeling by identifying the body language, the sooner you will be able to do something about it and reverse life's unwanted reactive experiences. The next time a stressor comes into your life, pay attention to what your body is saying.

Of course, there are exceptions to expressive symptoms. When the body is purging and releasing toxins it may appear sick when in fact it is doing the exact thing it's designed to do and that is to maintain homeostasis.

For the purpose of this exercise, I am specifically referring to the observations of the body language when actual stressful situations are at hand, and/or the emotion is actually taking place.

People of different temperaments are predisposed to different body messages because of our individuality. However, the places within your body that are consistently sensitive are trying to tell you something.

To have control over yourself, it's important to identify its messages when there is an inside or outside stimuli. Soon you will discover more and more how the body talks to you when you identify both the comfort zone and being out of that comfort zone.

When you learn to read these body messages, you will be able to ask yourself the following questions:

WHAT JUST OCCURRED WHEN I HAD THE STRESSFUL FEELING?

DO I FREQUENTLY FIND MYSELF PLACING MY HANDS OVER MY HEART, MY STOMACH, OR SOME OTHER PART OF THE BODY?

WHAT BODY PART WAS USED TO REFLECT THE FEELING?

WHAT WAS IT SAYING TO ME?

Pay attention to the words you say when you describe an irritation while under stress or being upset.

> "If you would see a person's soul, look at his body."
> Ralph Waldo Emerson
> *There is a reflection in the outer of what is in the inner.*

> "Disturbance brings other senses into action, and as wisdom is developed it gives man a knowledge of himself above the natural man of five senses.
> Phineas P. Quimby
> *An inner knowingness, an intuition, begins to speak to us, which can tell us more than the senses of taste, touch, sight, smell and hearing.*

> "…by repeated experiences, deliver us more and more completely out of the region of anxious thought and toilsome labour and bring us into a new world where the useful employment of all our powers, whether mental or physical, will only be an unfolding of our individuality upon the lives of its own nature, and therefore a perpetual source of health and happiness…"
>
> Thomas Troward
>
> *Let us learn from our experiences so that we may arise and come forth as a new individual. This unfoldment will reveal our true nature. Be healthy and happy.*

> "Every chronic problem has a mental component."
>
> Dr. Mary B. Anderson, D.C.
>
> *When problems keep repeating itself, it's time to pay attention to what is being said. What's the message?*

> "When I want to understand what is happening today or try to decide what will happen tomorrow, I look back."
>
> Oliver Wendell Holmes, Jr.
>
> *Reflecting on your past history and what was the end result can help us make changes in our lives. I like the expression: IDTA ("I did that already.")*

> "Memory at the conscious level is influenced by thoughts that can initiate defense physiology and be the stimulus to the sensory system."
>
> Dr. M. T. Morter, Jr., D.C.
>
> *Scientific studies have determined that continued memory influences our physiology. Why not record happy, peaceful and loving thoughts in our mind in order to stimulate love?*

HOW TO TALK TO YOURSELF

In this chapter, after introspection we see that we cannot run away from ourselves no matter where we go, and our body is expressing a language all of its own. Now we have to learn day by day, moment by moment, a new way to communicate with our inner self. Having an understanding that thoughts are things, focus on the idea that we are creating our world and our life's experiences by what we are saying to ourselves.

LOOK AT YOURSELF IN THE MIRROR AND SAY,
"WHO AM I?"
What response do you get? Write it down:

NOW IMAGINE TAKING A LAYER OFF OF YOURSELF AND GO A LITTLE DEEPER TO ASK THE SAME QUESTION.
"WHO AM I?" *Write it down.*

As you continue to peel back the layers of who you are, eventually it will lead back to the essence of your original Self. Call it whatever you like. **I prefer to say, "I am an Intelligence, which is part of an all-encompassing creative Universal Intelligence. Being part of this original Intelligence makes me a co-creator. What I think and say makes me who I am."** Everything is recorded in that subconscious part of you.

I often heard people say, "Well, I thought and said so many negative things how can I ever get out of this mess I'm in."

Picture a scale of justice. One side has all the negative thoughts recorded to date and the other side has all the positive thoughts recorded to date.

Right now the scale may be tipped on one side more than the other. If weighing your negative thinking may have made the scale heavier on one side, all is not lost. We can still offset the scale by changing our thinking to be positive. This eventually will cause the scale to tip in the other direction. It may take time, but with persistence, the scales will change and with it so will your life.

> "Trained thought is far more powerful than untrained thought."
> Ernest Holmes
>
> *Form constructive positive thoughts.*

As individuals, every day, every moment, every second we have choices. Not only do we choose what we can think and say, we have the *right* to choose our thoughts and words.

Thoughts become things. A point to remember is that your mind activity inevitably creates its physical correspondent.

In learning how to talk to yourself, come to the realization that in the deepest innermost level of Innate Intelligence is where the essence of who you are resides. Being a co-creator with that Intelligence is the most powerful healing agency known to the mind of man. Separation from this thought is what gets us into "trouble".

> "Self suggestion makes you master of yourself."
> W. Clement Stone

HOW DO YOU VIEW YOURSELF AND YOUR RELATIONSHIP TO THIS INNATE INTELLIGENCE?

In a few words, write down what you feel rather what you believe.

If you do not feel a connection with your Innate Intelligence, what do you feel?

If you do feel a Oneness with this Innate Intelligence, what makes you feel separated at times?

If you have doubts about yourself, try internalizing the following statements:

I HAVE ALWAYS KNOWN THE TRUTH OF
    MY INNER VOICE.
NO FEAR OR DOUBT CAN KEEP MY INNER
    KNOWLEDGE FROM ME.
MY INTUITIVE WISDOM COMES FROM WITHIN.
I EXPRESS THIS WISDOM DAILY.

By keeping these thoughts in mind you are identifying yourself with a Truth that can set you free. But, more than that, understanding and identifying with this Innate Intelligence gives more meaning to why or how affirmations can be powerful statements. They are not just words that sound good. They are powerful words. They have the power to create.

Now take a second look and dissect these common expressions.

"I ALWAYS SEEM TO GET A HEADACHE WHEN..."
"I WISH SHE'D GET OFF MY BACK."
"I CAN'T GET THIS OFF OF MY CHEST."
"MY FOOT ALWAYS HURTS"
"I'M SO SICK AND TIRED OF EVERYTHING."

By allowing yourself to replace words with a positive self-suggestion, starts to record a new tape in your subconscious mind. Another method is to just release the thought altogether. Say to yourself, "Release" or "Cancel". What is important is to momentarily step outside of your ego to release what you have just spoken and come from a place of your Innate Intelligence.

There is a part of you that knows that it knows and it's up to you to talk to yourself on that level. The more you identify with this knowingness and speak to your subconscious mind, it becomes a more conscious thought and the scale will tip in the other direction.

Reflect now to this very first question asked in the beginning of this exercise.

WHAT THOUGHTS ROUTINELY OCCUPY YOUR THINKING?

PART III – SELF-TALK

- *From a new place in thinking, I want you to write down in your notebook, without reservation, what you would like to envision routinely instead of what the appearances are reflecting. List the changes you want to happen in your life.*

- *Keep a journal to monitor your progress. The benefits of journaling helps one to stay focused and to see patterns in your life that your Innate Intelligence wants you to know. Take notes on what comes up for you in the Pick-of-the-Day! card.*

Don't give up. We don't stop eating and sleeping every day, and we don't stop thinking every day! But, how much time is spent thinking about our connection with Innate, which allows us to co-create our life's experiences in a powerful direction? Set aside a time each day, preferably the same time everyday and internalize your Oneness with that Innate Intelligence for clarity, guidance, direction and wisdom.

Make the commitment now and write the following in your notebook:

I commit to _____ every day to the Truth that sets me free.
    (Amount of time)

Date:_____**Signed:**_____

*Whether you set a quiet time of 5, 10, 15 minutes, 1 hr. or whatever, speak to yourself, and then **listen** to that inner Wisdom. This conversation may be the most important commitment of your life.*

> "A change in what we tell ourselves will result in a change in our behavior. Positive, repetitive self-talk...changes our self-image, and the suggestions we offer to ourselves...will be expressed in our actions. What we impress upon our minds, we inevitably become."
> — Author Unknown

> "Your self-image is your pattern! Every thought has an activity visualized. Every activity belongs to a pattern. You identify with your pattern or thought. Your pattern leads your life."
> — J. G. Gallimore

> "We cannot always control our thoughts, but we can control our words, and repetition impresses the subconscious, and we are then master of the situation."
> — Florence Scovel Shinn

> "To come to be, you must have a vision of Being, a Dream, a Purpose, a Principle. You will become what your vision is...."
> — Peter Nivio Zarlenga

> "If you wish to know the road up the mountain, ask the man who goes back and forth on it."
> — Zenrin

Zenrin's quote, for me personally, had much power associated with it. It was one of the motivations prompting me to write this book and inspire others to travel their own road.

As this chapter closes, adopt what it means to be at peace with your own Innate Self, which is an offspring of the ultimate Universal Intelligence. It doesn't matter what you name it. All that matters is to live in peace with your true Self.

FINAL NOTE

By doing this exercise only once, it would be just a mere introduction to changing your life.

Take inventory often.

Acknowledgements

The topics in this book are written because of the encouragement of the many patients and individuals who have asked for my services. There are also doctors, ministers and friends, who share a similar fundamental belief in the principle that the still small voice within has an Innate Intelligence and is a co-creator with Universal Intelligence.

I would like to express my gratitude to Tiffany Porter, PhD and Dale Strack for supporting me with ideas, consulting and editing. A special thanks to Paul Lloyd Warner for typesetting and cover design.

To those who are and have been influential in my life, I would like to applaud Dr. John Bohan, DC, Dr. Ronald C. Pluese, DC, and Rev. Dr. Sharron Stroud.

For the re-enforcement of my belief in the philosophy of an Innate Intelligence within, I wish to recognize my alma mater, Logan College of Chiropractic, Seaside Center for Spiritual Living and any and all like-minded personal groups and associations.

I want to acknowledge my spouse, Don and my sons, Richard, Dennis and Steve, as well as Rev. Christian Sorensen, DD, Lesley Deluz, PhD, Mary Meyer, RN/NP, Arlene Bender, Jean

Raymond, and Bette Statton who continue to witness my strong conviction in this Innate Wisdom and the role it plays in my life.

And in memory of my personal assistant for many years of dedicated service and unconditional love … "Sammy, the therapy dog extraordinaire".

Bibliography

Brophy, Thomas G,, Ph.D. 1999. *The Mechanism Demands a Mysticism, An Exploration of Spirit, Matter and Physics.* Blue Hill, Medicine Bear Publishing.

Cleary, Thomas. 1993. *The Essential Confucius. The Heart of Confucius' Teachings In Authentic I Ching Order.* San Francisco CA: Harper San Francisco, A Division of Harper Collings Publishers.

Dass, Ram. 1978. *Journey of Awakening: A Meditator's Guidebook.* A Bantam Book.

Easwaran, Eknath. 1992. *The Dhammapada, Translated for the Modern Reader.* Nilgiri Press, Tomales, California. Fourth Printing.

Greene, Brian. 2000. *The Elegant Universe. Superstrings, Hidden Dimensions, and the Quest for the Ultimate Theory.* New York: Vintage Books. A Division of Random House, Inc.

Holmes, Ernest. 1938. *The Science of Mind.* New York: Dodd, Mead and Company

Lipton, Bruce, Ph.D. 2005. *The Biology of Belief: Unleashing the Power of Consciousness, Matter and Miracles.* Santa Rosa, CA: Mountain of Love/Elite Books.

Newberg, Andrew, M.D., Eugene D'Aguili, M.D., Ph.D. and Vince Rause. 2001. *Why God Won't Go Away, Brain Science and the Biology of Belief.* New York: Ballantine Books.

Sapolsky, Robert M. 1998. *Why Zebras Don't Get Ulcers. An Updated Guide to Stress, Stress-Related Disease, and Coping.* New York: W. H. Freeman and Company

Zohar, Danah. 1990. *The Quantum Self. Human Nature and Consciousness Defined by the New Physics.* New York: William Morrow and Company, Inc.

Disclaimer

The introspection of each person is unique to the self. This book has been written to share the similarities perceived and observed from thousands of people that I have encountered, and who have realized that their recurrent life conditions and physical health contain a mental and/or emotional component. After understanding and accepting that there is an Innate Intelligence that guides and directs, lives have had favorable changes. It certainly has changed my life. The purpose here is to help others seek self-help by listening to their own still small voice. The author and publisher cannot guarantee results because results can only come from within yourself. Therefore, outcomes will vary depending on an understanding of what is real in conventional thinking and what is real as a result of an Innate Wisdom.

ORDER FORM
PICK-OF-THE-DAY!
Life is like a game and it's all about how to Innately play it!
By Dr. Mary B. Anderson

____Home study course book @ $21.95 ea.   _____

____Pick-of-the Day! cards @ $10.95 per deck   _____

CA residents add 8.75% Sales Tax   _____

Shipping & Handling add $10.00 for book, only   _____

Shipping & Handling add $12.00 for book and cards, complete _____

Shipping & Handling add $5.00 for deck of cards, only   _____

                Total Amount_____

Send check or money order to:

      Treasures…from mary
   P. O. Box 231653, Encinitas CA 92023

Or you can visit the website at **www.TreasuresFromMary.com**
Phone orders call **760-298-3563.**

Master Card or Visa accepted (Circle one)

Card #_____Exp.Date:_____Sec. code_____

Name as it appears on the card:_____

Billing address;_____

City:_____State:_____Zip_____

Signature:_____Phone:_____

Shipping address: ☐ Same as above

Name:_____

Address:_____

City:_____State:_____Zip_____

ORDER FORM
PICK-OF-THE-DAY!
Life is like a game and it's all about how to Innately play it!
By Dr. Mary B. Anderson

____Home study course book @ $21.95 ea.   _____

____Pick-of-the Day! cards @ $10.95 per deck   _____

CA residents add 8.75% Sales Tax   _____

Shipping & Handling add $10.00 for book, only   _____

Shipping & Handling add $12.00 for book and cards, complete _____

Shipping & Handling add $5.00 for deck of cards, only   _____

Total Amount_____

Send check or money order to:

Treasures…from mary
P. O. Box 231653, Encinitas CA 92023

Or you can visit the website at **www.TreasuresFromMary.com**
Phone orders call **760-298-3563.**

Master Card or Visa accepted (Circle one)

Card #_____Exp.Date:_____ Sec. code_____

Name as it appears on the card:_____

Billing address;_____

City:_____State:_____Zip_____

Signature:_____Phone:_____

Shipping address: ☐ Same as above

Name:_____

Address:_____

City:_____State:_____Zip_____

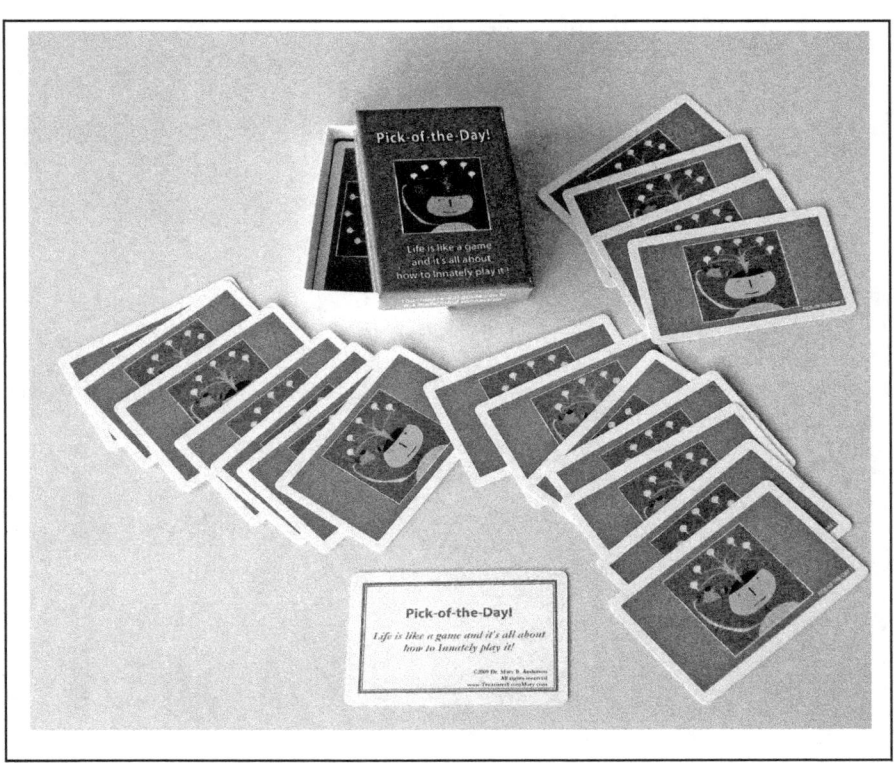

The 31 card deck is designed to assist you in daily self-empowerment.
Turn your activities into long-lasting results.
The card deck is in full color. Laminated and durable.
Sturdy box with lid. 2 ¼" x 3 ½" (Bridge Size Deck)
Printed in the U.S.A.
Order your deck today by using the order form or visit
www.TreasuresFromMary.com